Reading Rescue 1-2-3

RAISE YOUR CHILD'S READING LEVEL

2 GRADES THROUGH THIS SIMPLE

3-STEP PROGRAM

Peggy M. Wilber

Illustrations by Charles Stubbs

Prima Publishing
3000 Lava Ridge Court ❦ Roseville, California 95661
(800) 632-8676 ❦ www.primalifestyles.com

PRIMA PUBLISHING and colophon are trademarks of Prima Communications Inc., registered with the United States Patent and Trademark Office.

Names have been changed to protect the privacy of the individuals involved.

"One Hundred Most Frequent Words Found in Print," originally listed in *Reading Teacher's Book of Lists* by Edward Fry, © 1993 reprinted with permission of Prentice Hall Direct.

Interior design by Andrew Ogus

Library of Congress Cataloging-in-Publication Data
Wilber, Peggy M.
    Reading rescue 1-2-3 : raise your child's reading level 2 grades through this simple 3-step program / Peggy M. Wilber.
        p. cm.
    Includes bibliographical references and index.
    ISBN 0-7615-2963-2
    1. Reading—Parent participation. 2. Reading (Elementary) 3. Reading—Remedial teaching. 4. Children—Books and reading. I. Title: Reading rescue one-two-three. II. Title.
LB1573.W538 2000
649'58—dc21   00-057439

00 01 02 03 II 10 9 8 7 6 5 4 3 2 1

Printed in the United States of America

How to Order
Single copies may be ordered from Prima Publishing, 3000 Lava Ridge Court, Roseville, CA 95661; telephone (800) 632-8676, ext. 4444. Quantity discounts are also available. On your letterhead, include information concerning the intended use of the books and the number of books you wish to purchase.

Visit us online at www.primalifestyles.com

"A teacher affects eternity."
—Henry Brooks Adams

CONTENTS

ACKNOWLEDGMENTS

My most sincere and profound gratitude goes to Dr. Barbara E.R. Swaby, professor of education and the director of the graduate reading program at the University of Colorado at Colorado Springs. She teaches with both passion and excellence. Dr. Swaby's emphasis that every child is valuable and should receive appropriate instruction is pivotal in her teaching. Her concepts, theories, research, and practical application are foundational to this manuscript.

This book has been made possible by the support and efforts of both my family and friends. As the African proverb says, "It takes a village to raise a child." In this case, it took a caring community to help create this book.

My husband and children were patient and encouraging during my countless hours of writing. I love them and am thrilled to be fully a family member once again.

Marianne Hering contributed untold hours—editing the book proposal and answering numerous questions about publishing. This project would never have left the starting gate without her expertise and help. Donita Tompkins cheerfully edited and kept me true to the vision.

Mark Morehead patiently gave me step-by-step assistance to keep my computer working, and Debbie Morehead generously created and maintains my Web site. My parents, Drs. Jim and Jean Morehead, proofread the text and took my children on many wonderful outings.

Many thanks go to the members of Faith Evangelical Covenant Church, who encouraged David Olson, Brenda McCreight, and me to bring the Pikes Peak One+One Tutoring Program to fruition. Their continued support gives local children the opportunity of a lifetime— to learn to read.

The information in this book has been kid-tested, tutor-tested, and parent-tested by families and tutors who have been involved in the Pikes Peak One+One program. My appreciation goes to the many tutors, parents, teachers, and fabulous children who have passed through the One+One Program.

Other individuals have been more helpful than I can describe: Brenda McCreight, Bridget Mosley, Quinetta Wilson, Wil Biggs, Mary Wilber, and Millie Galyen.

Librarians worth their weight in gold include Vicki Fox, manager of Pikes Peak Library District Children's Services; the reference librarians of the Pikes Peak Library District; as well as Laurie Perkins and Katheryn DeRogatis.

I greatly appreciate the editors at Prima Publishing—Jamie Miller, acquisitions editor, and Andi Reese Brady, senior project editor. Their guidance and professional care from the beginning to the end has made the production of this book a great experience.

To the parent, grandparent, teacher, or friend who recognizes that a child is struggling in learning to read and responds by caring enough to spend time and energy rescuing this child in reading: Please know that you are making a profound difference in your child's life.

You are truly affecting the future.

INTRODUCTION

Shannon needed to be rescued in reading, and her mom was desperate. When I first met Shannon, a curtain of hair was covering her eyes, and she held onto Mom's hand like a C-clamp.

Based on first-grade testing results, teachers cautioned Shannon's mom that her daughter was dyslexic, had less than average intelligence, and would likely never learn to read. Mom, who believed in "Never say never," brought her to me for testing.

During the test, Shannon mentioned some facts about insects. *Hmm,* I thought. Even though she didn't know the alphabet, I knew there was a spark inside. I began to teach Mom, a single parent, skills she would need to rescue Shannon from a lifetime of illiteracy.

Is Shannon a rare occurrence in American children? Unfortunately, no. National tests show that 38 percent of fourth graders are unable to read at a basic level.[1] This adds up to ten million elementary aged children who can't read well.[2]

Girls have reading problems at the same rate as boys. But boys are identified as being reading disabled more often due to their lively behavior in the classroom.[3]

National tests show that 38 percent of fourth graders are unable to read at a basic level. This adds up to ten million elementary aged children who can't read well.

If you suspect that your child struggles in reading, here are some red flags to watch for:

- Does your child avoid reading—even cleaning her room instead?

- Does he cry or pout when you give him something to read?

- Is she unable to read McDonald's Happy Meal bags, Wendy's menus, or "Lost My Cat" signs?

- Does his reading sound labored, bumpy, and worse than his younger siblings or peers?

- Does she have trouble doing homework assignments by herself?

- After reading a selection, is he unable to tell you what it said?

- Do you have the feeling that she seems to be "lazy" or "unmotivated" in reading?

- Has he been labeled as having *dyslexia,* or *learning disabilities,* or *ADD?*

Three-fourths of children with reading difficulties in third grade will be poor readers in high school.[4] But 90 to 95 percent of third-grade children *who receive proper intervention* become able to read at grade level.[5]

Who will provide the necessary intervention? You may think it's the school's job. But let's say your child is in a classroom of twenty-five children. If eight of them have serious reading difficulties, how is the teacher going to address their needs during a half-hour daily reading period? At best these children will each receive only a few minutes of personalized instruction.

The problem is bigger than lack of time. You might think learning to read is the same as science or history—the teacher teaches, and children memorize facts to get A's. Unfortunately, it's not like that at all! Learning to read can be thwarted in many ways: Some children don't know the sounds of *t, a,* and *c.* Some know sounds but can't put them together to read *cat.* There are children who read lists of words—*a give bone dog*—but can't read: *give a dog a bone.* Other children invent words—*mokipple* or *calfen,* for example—and still others read in a monotone without comprehending. Just when I think I've seen every reading enigma, another child shows up with a new twist on reading difficulties.

The English language doesn't help at all. About half the words that we read follow easy phonic rules. The other half either break rules or follow more complex rules.[6] Many children can't apply complex phonic rules while reading.[7]

An important factor affecting children's reading success is auditory issues.[8] Some children can't *hear* differences between pairs of letter sounds *f, v* (*f* as in fish, *v* as in violin) or *b, p* (*b* as in boat, *p* as in pizza). Phonic skills are difficult to learn until they can process language sounds better. These same children can't pull words apart into distinct sounds. For example, instead of knowing that *d-o-g* makes *dog*, they think *dog* is a single unit. How are they going to understand sounding out words?

Who will rescue your child?

You will!

You already have the most important tool to teach your child—the ability to read. Reading intervention is not difficult, but it does require thirty minutes of time each day. Your home is the perfect setting for reading practice, and you are already motivated to help your child. *Reading Rescue 1-2-3* gives you easy-to-apply, hands-on information. It's a complete manual with auditory games, phonic sheets to help connect sounds to letters, and stories for your child to practice reading.

A friend from church called. Her daughter Anika, a first-grader, could read her name and the words "the" and "said." Period. She knew few alphabet letters, much less any of their sounds. Worst of all, she *hated* reading. Mom wanted me to tutor Anika to get her back on track.

I made a counterproposal to Anika's mom. "Bring her over to my house, and I'll show *you* how to help her in reading." Mom agreed, and we decided on 2:00 P.M. After getting off the phone, I went upstairs to choose a good book, paper and a pencil, and some jungle animal stickers. My goals were that Anika would go from drowning in an ocean of "undecodable" words to swimming in the wonderful world of cobras or Komodo Dragons, *and* that Anika and her mom would have fun in the process.

I used to tutor children. It was lots of fun watching them improve in reading skills. Then there became too many children. Parents I had never met called, and there weren't enough hours of sunshine to meet

Children who received a daily half hour of instruction surged forward in reading skills—sometimes up to two reading levels per semester.

the demand. The question became, "How could I transfer my knowledge to other people?"

I began a tutoring program at church, using volunteers I had trained. We tutored twenty-five children every Tuesday night. The tutors were grandmothers, teenage girls, salesmen, and Air Force retirees—every last one of them doing a great job. Students they tutored gained one or two reading levels per year.

But couldn't we do better? I realized that parents were an untapped resource; they were with their kids every night of the week, and that beats one hour every seven days. So I created training sessions for parents (also grandparents, older siblings, and daycare providers). Even the most reluctant, "not sure I'm qualified" parents experienced success working with their children.

Children who received a daily half hour of instruction surged forward in reading skills—sometimes up to two reading levels per semester. Their attitudes improved from "I hate reading" to "Listen to this, Mom!" The children's self-esteem rose, and of course, their grades did too.

Reading Rescue 1-2-3 is an extension of those training sessions. It has been parent- and kid-tested. It puts into your hands all the materials you need to help your child learn to read. Just as Anika's mom helped her, you will rescue your child from a lifetime of poor literacy.

Remember Shannon? Three semesters later, her eyes glow when she talks about mosquitoes and stinkbugs. She reads at grade level and does her homework unassisted. Best of all, her teachers no longer mention dyslexia or low I.Q. to her mom.

Take this book in hand, pull up two chairs, and begin rescuing your child in reading. It will be sweet music to your ears when one day your child says to you, "Did you know that elephants are tusk-handed? It says right here that one tusk is longer than the other because the elephant uses it more . . ."

PART I

Rescuing Your Child

What Every Parent Needs to Know

Portrait of a Rescuing Parent

Beverly called to talk with me about her second-grade daughter, Cara, who was behind in reading skills. Beverly was scheduled to meet with Cara's school teacher, special education teacher, and principal to form an Individualized Education Plan, or IEP, which mandates what special education services a child needs and how to provide them. The special education teacher had told Beverly, "I think Cara needs to come to the IEP meeting. We're going to talk to her about her lack of motivation. Cara's problem is that she's lazy. If she worked harder, she would get better grades."

I advised Beverly not to bring her daughter to the IEP meeting. Those comments could crush a child's spirit. We talked about factors affecting Cara's school performance. Beverly decided to schedule vision and pediatric appointments for additional testing. It turned out that Cara needed eyeglasses. She was diagnosed with a sensory modulation disorder, which meant that she was dozing with her eyes open in school, and she had low muscle tone.

Cara began receiving six months of therapy to learn self-monitoring and brain-arousal techniques. She got help from special education teachers in school. Beverly took my parent training seminar and worked with Cara a half hour every night on reading skills.

What a difference those adjustments made! Cara is now in fifth grade and no longer needs special education services. She's reading at grade level, and her grades are good. Spurred by Cara's needs, Beverly went the extra mile and rescued her daughter.

CHAPTER 1

Steps into Reading

The Definition of Reading

The only thing you did to help your child learn to walk was hold his chubby hand. Oh, perhaps you bought a pair of shoes with ankle supports to help him balance. But basically he learned to walk by himself, following an internal program as fixed as the sun's rising.

Reading isn't like learning to walk or talk. It doesn't occur naturally—although it seems that way for some children. However, based on huge numbers of normal children who can't read, we know it's not automatic.[1] You need to do more than hold your child's hand, read Dr. Seuss books to him, and wait for the sun to shine.

Consider Sam, who read a story to me: "Ab-ra-ham L-in-c-oln was Pr-Pres-s-i-d-ent du-ring th-e C-iv-il W-ar." He labored over every word. Was this reading? Not really—he "called the words," but he needs help.

Five Components

Every child must master five components to become a good reader:

1. *Phonological Awareness*—hearing and manipulating the sounds of language.
2. *Phonics*—learning how to attach sounds to alphabet letters.
3. *Sight Words*—memorizing words that don't follow easy phonic rules.
4. *Fluency*—reading smoothly at the speed that a person talks.

5. *Comprehension*—understanding what was read, which is the entire purpose for reading.

All five components are necessary. It's not enough to know phonics. Knowing both phonics and sight words doesn't guarantee fluency. Even being able to read out loud doesn't always lead to comprehension.

A child who can't read is intelligent, but his brain is wired differently. He needs direct instruction to become a good reader. So how do you help him learn to read? You work with him on each of the five important components. Let's look at them again.

Phonological Awareness: An Ear/Brain Connection

Phonological awareness is the understanding that *sounds* of speech can be broken apart. It begins with hearing separate words that make up sentences: "Can-I-have-a-hot-dog-for-supper?" to hearing syllables inside of words: "in-ter-est-ing," and sounds that make up "w-or-d-s." It is also being able to rhyme: "bug-dug-rug."

Learning how to read begins in your child's ears. You probably thought it was through your child's eyes! But his ears and brain have to be well connected before your child can learn to read. Every time you talk, sing, or read to your child, you are laying an auditory foundation for his success in reading.[2] Playing auditory games will help improve his phonological awareness.

Phonics

Phonics is attaching sounds to letters. Letter names are different from letter sounds. Letter *a* says "aah" as in apple, and letter *b* says "b" as in boat, and so on. Most children who can't read well don't know the short vowel (*a, e, i, o, u*) sounds. Short vowels are hard to remember because they sound so much alike. A child must learn phonic information to the point of becoming automatic—remembering letter

Learning to read begins in your child's ears, not his eyes.

sounds instantaneously. Otherwise, it could take him hours to read a story.

Sight Words

Have you ever thought about the word *eight, brought,* or *know?* These words follow complicated phonic rules. It's more efficient for your child to memorize them as sight words.

A great way for your child to learn sight words is to read lots of "connected print." Connected print is stories and information found in books or magazines. It's very different from worksheets or lists of spelling words. Whole language proponents are correct in saying that children should spend time every day reading books, rather than doing tons of worksheets, which aren't connected print, and don't really provide reading practice.

Fluency

Fluency is reading smoothly, with expression, at the same speed that your child talks—not just saying the words fast.

A nonfluent reader spends his energy decoding words. Ted read this sentence in a monotone, "A sn-ak, sn-ake w-e-nt d-o d-ow-n a h-ole." When he finished, he'd forgotten what the sentence was about. Nonfluent reading blocks comprehension because it's so slow and fragmented that short-term memory can't hold it. A fluent reader reads in phrases, allowing his brain to retain lots more information.

Two techniques will help improve your child's fluency: Choose reading selections that aren't too hard for him to read and help him reread short selections to excellence. These will be discussed further in a later chapter.

Two techniques will help improve your child's fluency: Choose reading selections that aren't too hard for him to read and help him reread short selections to excellence.

Comprehension, the Goal

My friend's first-grade son was sitting at my table. His mom said, "Read something to Mrs. Wilber." He read a story slowly to me and it sounded pretty good. I asked him "What was the story about?" He said, "I don't know." He worked so hard to call the words that he wasn't able to pay attention to the plot. This can happen to a beginning reader.

Language is made up of four categories: listening, talking, reading, and writing. Listening has the largest vocabulary, and writing has the smallest.[3]

listening	talking	reading	writing
largest vocabulary	←	→	smallest vocabulary

When the listening vocabulary increases, this expands the other three language vocabularies. You didn't know that reading *Fox in Socks* to your child had such potential, did you?

There are lots of things to read to your child: poetry, stories, cartoons, and even back panels of cereal boxes. When you read a selection to your child, you are putting new vocabulary words and new ideas into his ears.

Emil liked to read books about whales living in the ocean. When he first saw the word *ocean,* he was able to make a good guess and say "ocean" instead of saying "occasion" or "only." The vocabulary stored in his brain helped him every time he sat down to read.

I must have read *"Stand Back," Said the Elephant, "I'm Going to Sneeze!"* forty times to my daughter. She liked the sneeze part. She was able to join me by saying sections from memory. Parents often worry that "memorizing" a book is not reading. In fact, it facilitates reading.

Children often ask for the same book to be read over and over. After the fifteenth time, you may be bored, but you are creating important language pathways in your child's brain. Repeated readings help build a sense of story, and predict what might happen next. Prediction is a major skill of comprehension.

I still read to my twelve-year-old daughter and eight-year-old son each day. Every child, no matter how old, benefits from listening to *Aesop Fables* or *Ranger Rick* articles.

Learning to Read and Reading to Learn

Your child's main window of opportunity to *learn to read* in school happens in kindergarten through third grade. His teachers provide reading instruction, reading materials, and reading practice during these four years. Then he'll go through a quick transition at the beginning of fourth grade to *reading to learn*.

From fourth grade on, it's expected that your child will learn new information by himself—from science, social studies, math, and language textbooks, as well as other written materials. Successful readers enjoy a smooth transition from *learning to read* to *reading to learn*. We want your child to enjoy the same transition.

An upper elementary student who is beyond the "opportunity window" is also able to learn to read, but remediation resources in school are more limited. He will need your help doing activities in this book to become a successful reader.

No matter your child's age, or his grade level, today is the day to begin helping him learn to read better. When your child becomes proficient in all five categories—phonological awareness, phonics, sight words, fluency, and comprehension—he will make strides in reading as he does in walking.

Information to Remember

○ Learning how to read begins in your child's ears.

○ Read lots of different books to your child to increase his vocabulary and concepts.

○ Phonological awareness, phonics, sight words, and fluency are major skills of reading.

○ Comprehension is the ultimate goal of reading.

CHAPTER 2

High Hurdles

Children Who Aren't Reading

Maria is at the starting line. The pistol fires and she begins to run. Rising before her, at nose-height, are hurdles. Other children bound over them. Maria backs up and leaps, catching her toes on a hurdle as she goes over. She lands face first in the dust. For Maria, running this race is no fun.

Some children face hurdles on the path to reading. Why are they slowed down, but not others? There are a number of possible factors, many of which are easy to fix. Let's look at recent discoveries about the brain.

It's All in Their Heads

Researchers have peeked inside the brains of children while they perform different reading tasks. Using a functional Magnetic Resonance Imaging (fMRI) machine, scientists have discovered differences in brain metabolism between children who read well and those who don't.[1]

During brain scans, the *language centers* of children who read well light up in spots, with lots of blood flowing. Other children have less blood flow in those centers, and also have greater difficulty doing reading tasks.[2]

Difficulty in reading seems to be an inheritable trait. You may know someone in your family who struggles in reading. Here's the good news: scientists believe that the genetic effects are weak—they *can* be overridden by good instruction that you provide.[3]

Instruction doesn't have to be tedious to be effective. Playing auditory games (see chapters 9 and 13) five minutes a day will help the language centers of your child's brain light up brighter than a Christmas tree.

Hearing, Speech Impediments

When Rachael was a baby, she had a lot of ear infections. Her mom didn't realize she wasn't hearing well. The doctor finally put tubes in Rachael's ears, but she had lost valuable time when she wasn't hearing sounds of the English language clearly.

When a child is born, she listens to sounds around her. If her ears are filled with fluid due to ear infections, the quality of sounds she hears is affected. If your child speaks unclearly, she is repeating distorted sounds of the English language. These factors (ear infections and speech issues) may affect her ability to hear differences between letter sounds.[4]

"Jamie, do these two words sound the same or different? *big-dig,*" asked her teacher.

"They sound the same," said Jamie.

"Now," said the teacher, "look at my mouth when I say them: *big-dig.*"

"Oh," said Jamie, "They sound different."

In order to give the right answer, Jamie had to watch her teacher's mouth making the letter sounds.

I ask children to close their eyes and tell me if two letters sound the same or different. "Why is this important?" you may ask. Well, if your child can't hear differences in letter sounds, she won't be able to memorize them correctly.

Playing auditory games will prepare your prereading child's brain to learn phonic skills. In fact, all of your children will benefit from playing auditory games.

There are differing degrees of struggling with reading. Some children are slightly behind in reading skills. They need review and practice, and then they take off. Other children are further behind. In addition to auditory issues, children may encounter other hurdles in the path to reading. See if your child fits into any of the following categories.

Vision Deficiencies

As I was tutoring Adele one day, I noticed she tilted her head while reading. She also squinted. Mom said that Adele's eyes had recently been tested at school. *Hmmm.* We decided to send her to an optometrist. After checking Adele's eyes, the optometrist said that she needed a pair of reading glasses.

Vision problems are hard to detect. Does your child demonstrate any of these while reading?

- Lose her place or reread the same line
- Tilt her head or hold the book sideways
- Squint or rub her eyes
- Hold the book close or far away
- Complain of feeling tired or dizzy
- Have frequent headaches or sore eyes

These are not normal growing pains. They are important signals that need to be investigated.

A good optometrist will diagnose and remedy your child's visual needs. Some children have improved in reading after receiving vision therapy.[5] One benefit to wearing glasses, besides seeing more clearly, is that your child can read for longer periods of time before getting tired. As you can imagine, it's a lot easier to learn how to read when your eyes are working right.

More Than One Learning Style

My friend and I were drinking tea when her son came up from the basement. He was holding a fabulous boat made of Legos. Obviously, he liked to make things, but he was having trouble learning how to read. What was going on?

> *It's easier for children to learn when they are being taught using more than one style of activities.*

My friend's son was experiencing a mismatch between how he likes to learn and how he was being taught. Some children aren't wired to sit at desks doing multiple worksheets each day.

Does your child like to make things? Does she draw lots of pictures? Maybe she likes *I Spy* books or playing the drums. It's easier for children to learn when they are being taught using more than one style of activities.

Three major styles of learning are:

- *Visual*—These kids excel at Nintendo or computer games, and they remember what you wore yesterday.
- *Kinesthetic*—These children learn through touch and movement. They love karate, skateboarding, and other sports. They learn best when a movement activity is added to instruction.
- *Auditory*—These children like music, and remember things you said three months ago, even though you have long since forgotten.

Sometimes bright children, labeled as having Attention Deficit Disorders (ADD) or low I.Q., are being taught using auditory methods, when auditory is their weakest mode of learning. When they are taught using activities from more than one style of learning, all of a sudden their I.Q. seems to increase, and ADD behavior decreases.

Inability to Self-Prime

We all walk around with information stored in our brains. Information comes into our brains in two major ways: we pull it in by using our senses, asking questions, reading, and listening to people talk; *or* it is intentionally and directly taught to us.

Mrs. Chantal begins the morning reading discussion by saying, "Today we are going to read about Bengal tigers. Who can tell me something about tigers?"

Six children rapidly raise their hands to offer information.

"Yes, Ben?" says Mrs. Chantal.

"I think Bengal tigers live in India," says Ben.

"That's right," says Mrs. Chantal. "Yes, Stephanie?"

Stephanie says, "I read that every tiger has his own set of stripes, like my fingerprints."

Ben and Stephanie already have information called prior knowledge stored in their brains. They prime themselves by quickly retrieving information and are ready to *hook* more facts onto previous information. Our culture affirms children who quickly absorb information as being smart.

What about a child who has difficulty in reading? For one thing, it's the chicken-and-egg story—children who don't read well aren't getting as many new tidbits of information as are children who read a lot. They often have auditory processing issues and aren't gaining information through their ears as easily as other kids. Therefore they have less prior knowledge and fewer hooks for new incoming information.

I have found that poor readers ask fewer questions, have a weaker auditory memory, and make fewer connections between sets of information. In fact, they compartmentalize what they learn. For example, Sandra miscalled the word *bone:*

"Sandra, did you see letter *e* at the end of *bone?* It's bossy and makes the *o* in *bone* say its own name," I said. "Did you learn about silent *e* in school?"

Her eyes got big and she nodded, "Yeah, I did lots of silent *e* worksheets."

"This is when you need to *use* the silent *e* rule," I said.

"Oh," she said.

Sandra had completed worksheets but didn't know to apply silent *e* while reading. Silent *e* was sitting in one part of her brain, unused, while she was trying to read.

I am not for a minute implying that these children are stupid or lazy—because they're not. These children are also bright, but their brains have strengths in other areas.

Teach by Modeling

What's the best method to teach a child who can't self-prime? First of all, tell her *how* you know what you know. She looks at you and honestly believes that you were born knowing the difference between dolphins and porpoises and that carbon dioxide makes Pepsi fizz. She has no idea how you got information or how to get it for herself.

A good teacher doesn't leave anything up to happenstance. She *models*. She talks out loud while figuring out problems:

"When I see that in a picture I know . . ."

"I was wondering how this worked, so I looked it up in the encyclopedia . . ."

"I couldn't remember so I went back to page . . ."

"In order to remember that, I made a picture inside my head . . ."

In every way, she models for children how to find and remember information.

We need to be teaching these children using a "show and tell" method of instruction. We can't just "tell," because they don't absorb auditory information very well. We must make connections *for* them. Over time, with practice, they will learn to make their own connections.

Every time you teach something new, remind your child of an old piece of information on which to hook new information. Teach new information using a visual and auditory style, *and* if possible in a kinesthetic style. The new piece of information will hang on a hook in her brain, ready for application.

Dad said, "Terri, remember when we went to the lake and saw ducks swimming around?"

"Yes," said Terri. "And we fed them bread crumbs."

"That's right," said Dad. "We saw a few ducks flying and making skid landings on the lake."

"Yeah. I remember that," said Terri.

In every way, a good teacher models for children how to find and remember new information.

"Well, every year ducks lose their flying feathers. It takes a month for them to grow new ones. This is called molting. First, we're going to look at pictures in this book of ducks molting. Then we'll read about it."

The average child needs between four to fourteen exposures to learn a new fact. Others need more than twenty exposures.[6] When you feel frustrated because your child "isn't getting it," remember that she may need eleven to seventeen more explanations. Take a deep breath and consider making a new approach using a kinesthetic or visual activity.

To highlight visual, kinesthetic, and auditory activities in this book, I have placed

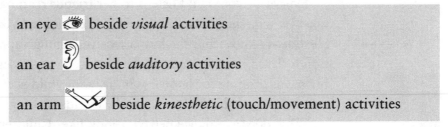

an eye beside *visual* activities

an ear beside *auditory* activities

an arm beside *kinesthetic* (touch/movement) activities

This will alert you to using multiple learning styles while working with your child.

Reading Avoidance

The first time I met Alan, he sat on a chair in a fetal position. His arms were wrapped around his legs. I held a book in front of him and he began to cry. He didn't want to read because he didn't want to experience more failure.

Many times a child misbehaves during reading activities because she is experiencing failure. Instead of punishing her behavior, I work on improving her reading skills. (I will address her misbehavior, too, but not in a punishing mode.) I have found that when a child begins to read better, her misbehavior disappears!

The average child needs between four to fourteen exposures to learn a new fact. Others need more than twenty exposures.

A child who can't read doesn't have the necessary tools to read well yet. Her inability to read is certainly not due to laziness!

Every once in awhile a parent says to me, "My daughter can't read because she's lazy." I don't agree with that opinion. A child who can't read doesn't have the necessary tools to read well *yet* or she is dealing with factors that block reading skills. Her inability to read is certainly not due to laziness! She is caught in a cycle—she can't read, so she avoids reading. Her friends surge ahead in reading skills leaving her in the dust.

Every day your child listens to her friends reading in class. "There must be something wrong with me," she thinks. "Maybe I'm stupid." She doesn't know that she hasn't received enough appropriate instruction to learn how to read. She might need eyeglasses and she probably needs training for her ears. Sadly, your child is convinced that she will never learn how to read, so she avoids reading.

What does avoidance behavior look like? Children exhibit all sorts of avoidance behavior such as pouting, crying, slouching, and talking excessively. They stall, tap their feet, cover their mouths with their hands, and do anything else in their power to avoid reading. One child told her mother, "Oh, I've already learned that," every time they sat down to work together. Does your child demonstrate any avoidance behaviors?

What do you do when faced with a task you don't like? You avoid it! It's amazing how the entire garage gets cleaned and organized before income tax forms are filled out. Sometimes we promise ourselves a little reward, such as a piece of chocolate to enjoy when the task is done. Little rewards can motivate your child also and help to decrease her avoidance behavior.

Looking at Labels

Have you noticed that I haven't used terms such as "dyslexia," "learning disabilities," "ADD," or "ADHD" very much? They are genuine diagnoses, affecting lots of children. However, they aren't an excuse. Remember that over 90 percent of children labeled as having dyslexia *can learn* to read at grade level with proper instruction. No matter what the label or diagnosis—go ahead, use this book, and teach your child to read.

Activities That Compete with Reading

Thousands of students were surveyed during testing in 1998. Students who watched less than three hours of television per day scored better than students who watched more TV. Students who read more each day had higher scores than students who read less.[7] These results suggest that children who read more, read better. Compare what you used to do as a child with your child's daily activities.

Over the next three days, tally up the time your child spends playing Nintendo and computer games, watching TV, and talking on the phone. These fun activities are taking the place of reading activities that you and I used to do when we were kids.

If you are serious about helping your child improve her reading skills, place a half hour of reading before her other activities. It will be the most valuable and important time that she spends each day!

Children who read books every day,
grow up to be smart in every way.

Information to Remember

- Your child might need a vision exam.
- She will benefit from doing reading activities using visual, auditory, and kinesthetic (touch/movement) styles of learning.
- Reading avoidance will decrease as her reading improves.
- Help your child to read every day.

CHAPTER 3

Ready to Read

The Game Plan

"I say what I mean and I mean what I say—I am NOT going to read any words today!"

—from *I Am Not Going to Read Any Words Today,* by Linda Hayward, Scholastic, 1995

Does your dining room table sometimes resemble a battlefield? Are there moans in the air? Do you find yourself shouting, "Why can't you get this right?" Does your child cry and throw pencils in the air? There is a battle of opposite goals going on: you want your child to practice reading and he wants to do anything but. Some children are passive; they stall or divert your attention. It doesn't look like a battle-field but there's a war going on—a war of wills. How do you get a child to read when he doesn't want to?

Adults who give children consistency and encouragement get the best results. Your child will work the hardest when you are encouraging and patient with him. These statements will keep your child's attitude above water:

- "Good try!"
- "Good job saying a word that begins with those first two letters."
- "You're working hard."

On the other hand, these words will close your child down like the hatch of a submarine ready to dive:

- "No! That's not the right word."
- "You know this word!"
- "You've already learned this."
- "Why can't you remember this?"

Please believe that your child is doing the best he can at this moment with the few tools he has inside of him. When he gets more tools, he will read (and behave) better.

Having a Game Plan

Consider yourself to be a coach of a winning team. Give pep talks so your child understands how to score reading goals:

"Justin, what is *your* goal in reading?" asked Mom.

"I want to read *Sports Illustrated for Kids,*" said Justin.

"Excellent!" said Mom. "What do you need to do so that can happen?"

Justin said, "I'll have to read every day?"

"Yes, and we're going to work on strategies to help you become a good reader," said Mom. "It'll be hard work but you'll feel proud when you're reading *Sports Illustrated*!"

Tell your child what's in it for him. Every child has something near and dear to his heart. Maybe he likes street hockey or airplanes. Get books from the library on his favorite topic. Tell him that someday he will be able to read these books by himself. For now, you are going to help him read these books. He'll be twice as likely to work hard towards a meaningful prize.

As a coach, you will choose short-term reading goals. At the beginning of each practice reading time, remind him of today's goal.

"Justin, every time you come to a word that you don't know, I want you to look at the first two letters, and get your mouth ready to say that sound. That'll be today's strategy. Every time you say the sound of the first two letters, I am going to put a check mark on this piece of paper. Can we get ten points today?" asked Mom.

He might need reminding or even re-instruction. Remember that children need between four and fourteen exposures to apply a new piece of information. That is a lot of repetition on your part. But it's how a child's brain works.

When your child does something well, give him encouragement and a hug. Use words to pat your child on the back:

- "You did a nice job with . . ."
- "I was impressed when you . . ."
- "You should feel proud about . . ."

Fill in the endings of the above sentences with concrete examples of what your child did right. This highlights behavior that you want to see again. Rejoice in the little victories as they happen, because they add up to success in reading.

As players practice, they steadily get better at a game. It's more effective to work half an hour every day of the week than to put in two hours on the weekend. Don't be "weekend warriors." You will wear out your child and probably lose your patience. Slow and steady will win the game.

Create Feelings of Success

When I was learning how to teach reading, I was paired with a third-grader named David. He was two years behind in reading skills. We met daily for tutoring. I was happy to be there, but he wasn't. My problem was that he didn't want to read.

Another problem was that my teacher was walking around to see how well I was doing. *Uh-oh. I needed to find a way to help him read.* I said to him, "David, every time I see you sitting up and working hard, I am going to put a check mark on this paper. Let's see if you can fill up this piece of paper." He liked that idea and we were off and running.

Children don't see the value of practicing something unpleasant today for the future reward—of knowing how to read. Give your child as much positive reinforcement as possible. You are replacing his bad memories of reading failure with good memories.

Instant rewards are great motivators.

Instant rewards are great motivators. My daughter and I went to the grocery store to pick out candy that she liked. This was only used in our "Practice Reading" time together. Every few minutes that she was working, I gave her an M&M to eat. She was willing to work hard for candy. Think of small items that will motivate your child, such as:

- M&M's, raisins, Cheez-its, or sweet cereal
- Check marks or stars on a card
- Pennies dropped into a jar for every few minutes of hard work
- Stickers on a daily chart

Instant rewards work better at this stage than long-term rewards such as a toy at the end of the week.

As your child experiences more success in reading, her avoidance behavior drops away and external rewards aren't as necessary. The pleasure of reading becomes its own reward. I'll never forget the day when the timer rang. Our tutoring time together was done, and David yelled, "No! We can't stop here. I want to find out what happens to Clifford!" Reading had become its own reward for him.

Create a Good Environment for Practice Reading Time

Paula called to her son, who was watching television, "Jay, it's time to do your reading."

Reluctantly Jay went over to the sofa, where his older brother was playing *Gameboy*. They began to wrestle.

"Mom, Jim is bugging me," said Jay. Paula came into the room.

"I told you to do your reading," she said.

"But Mom," said Jay, "I can't find any books."

"Where are your books?" asked Paula. Jim began to snicker.

"Jay's baby books are in the car," he said. They began wrestling again.

Through clenched teeth Paula said, "Jay, get your books now! Jim, go upstairs and do your homework."

Did you experience déjà vu reading this scenario? Organizing the environment ahead of time will keep you from standing in Paula's shoes. It will also help your child to get the most out of reading practice. This may not be his favorite fifteen minutes in the day, so gather necessary reading materials ahead of time. Choose a good working place such as a table or desk, and reduce distractions.

Adults are able to block out unwanted distractions. *Oprah* is on TV, the kids are playing *Battleship,* and the baby is crying in her crib. You are sitting on the sofa reading a couple pages of Stephen King's newest novel. Somehow your brain is able to turn off nonessential noises and focus on reading.

Many children are unable to do this. Their brains can't sort or inhibit incoming sounds.[1,2] It's as if they are wearing hearing aids that magnify sounds.

A child needs to put all his efforts into learning how to read. When sounds of noisy siblings or television are reduced, he is able to focus on reading. How about asking your other children to read books during those fifteen minutes? Everyone benefits!

Establish a Routine

A harder question to answer may be, "When can you work together every day?" Some families read in the morning before school. Others do reading right after supper. The important thing is to find a daily time and place that works best for your family.

Reading for Fun

There are two different types of reading together: reading for fun and Practice Reading Time. Fun reading is when you read books or magazines to your child, or he is reading his favorite books to you. It doesn't matter whether your child is lying down on a bed or sitting on a swing. He can read when he's on the bus, or in a car.

Fun reading should include nonfiction books as well as storybooks. Children love to read about alligators, tornadoes, and Michael Jordan.

Practice Reading Time

Practice Reading Time is different. During these fifteen minutes your child will be *learning* how to read. Don't hand him a book while saying "Here, do this," then walk away. He needs your direct help until he becomes a better reader.

When your child was a baby, you had to change his diapers. That was part of being a parent. Eventually he became potty-trained, and you didn't have to do that odiferous task any more. Expect to be intimately involved in your child's reading training. This effort on your part will eventually produce an independent reader.

During Practice Reading Time your child should be reading *connected print*. Remember: connected print is books or magazines—not worksheets or flash cards. Working on spelling words for homework isn't in this category.

Reading Position

When I tutor a new student, I always introduce the Reading Position:

"Ben, before we begin, I want you to sit in Reading Position."

I then model what Reading Position looks like. "I want you to sit up in the chair like this, and put your hands in your lap." When he begins to slouch, I gently remind him to get back into Reading Position.

Make sure that your child's hands are in his lap, not holding up his head, covering his mouth, or playing with a pencil. Tilt the book up instead of laying it flat on the table. This way your child can see the book and not be hunched over. He should be looking at words in the book and not elsewhere. This is the least tiring position for your child, and it helps his brain to do its best work.

Fun reading should include nonfiction books as well as storybooks. Children love to read about alligators, tornadoes, and Michael Jordan.

Your child will work harder knowing that Practice Reading Time will end when the timer rings.

A friend of mine told me that she read to her child every night. But her nine-year-old son had not yet learned to read. I asked her, "Where is he sitting when you are reading with him?"

She told me, "John is in the top bunk, and his brother is on the bottom bunk. I'm sitting in a chair."

She has the right idea in reading to her children every night. However, she isn't doing Practice Reading Time because her child can't even see the words while she's reading. Now they sit at a table to do Practice Reading Time together.

Materials Needed for Practice Reading Time

Practice Reading Time will be more effective if you have the following items on hand:

- A timer
- Reading selection
- Pencil and note cards
- Little rewards

A Timer

When you begin, turn a kitchen timer to fifteen minutes. It's a good amount of time for a young child to work on reading. Your child will work harder knowing that Practice Reading Time will end when the timer rings.

If your child is fooling around, quietly increase the lost minutes on the timer. He'll quickly understand that he must do fifteen minutes of good work.

Even though your child may be two to three years behind in reading skills, don't do a half hour of Practice Reading Time. If you lengthen the time, the quality of work will go down. It's better to work hard for fifteen minutes rather than do half an hour of mediocre work.

During these fifteen minutes, you are in control of the reading selection. You're the one who holds up the book. Your finger should run under the words while you or your child is reading. With your finger setting the pace, your child will learn to read smoothly, and he will become more fluent. When he makes a mistake, tap your finger under the word to let him know he should try reading the word again.

A few teachers frown on the use of a finger to keep place. They are not taking into account that children have visual issues. Some lose their place and others see words moving around a page. Use a blank note card or bookmark instead of your finger, if you want, to move under the words while reading.

Pencil and Note Cards

Keep three-by-five-inch note cards handy. When your child miscalls two or three words, write them on note cards, and teach them to him as sight words (see chapter 16).

The routine has been set, you have chosen a reading place, distractions have been reduced, and your child knows how to sit in Reading Position. He may not love the fifteen minutes of reading at first. Give him little treats for his efforts. Over time his reading will improve and your hard work will be rewarded.

Information to Remember

○ You are your child's coach. Give him encouragement and support.

○ Instant rewards are better than long-term rewards.

○ Rejoice in little victories; they will add up to success in reading.

○ Have your child sit in Reading Position beside you.

○ Read lots of nonfiction and fiction books together.

○ Do Practice Reading Time for fifteen minutes every day.

CHAPTER 4

Reading Selections

To, With, and By

At Marisa's first piano lesson, the teacher put a copy of *Für Elise* by Beethoven in front of her. "Today you are going to learn this," said her teacher. Marisa's stomach did a flip-flop as she stared at baffling black dots on the music page.

What did her teacher skip over? Marisa needed to learn how to read music. She needed to practice thousands of scales and play hundreds of easier songs building up to *Für Elise*. Learning how to read is similar to learning to play the piano. If you leap over the foundation, your child will be staring at *Stuart Little* with a clenched stomach.

The Right Selection for Your Child

Like the chair that Goldilocks sat in, reading selections can be too hard, too soft (easy), or just right for your child. Let's look at selection levels.

Independent Level. A child can read a selection on this level fluently with good expression, by herself, and have 95 to 100 percent accuracy. A quick way to determine readability is the 1:20 rule—your child should misread no more than *one* in every twenty words.[1] If she makes more mistakes than that, the selection is too hard. Abandon ship, and help her choose an easier selection to read by herself.

> *At the Instructional Level, the reader should make no more than two mistakes per twenty words.*

Instructional Level. At this level your child should have 90 to 95 percent accuracy. She should make no more than *one* or *two* mistakes per twenty words. You must give your child support such as using the *To, With, and By* technique (see page 31) for her to benefit from reading a selection on this level.

Frustration Level. At this level your child has less than 90 percent accuracy.[2] Making your child read a selection on her Frustration Level causes nonfluent reading, and is like putting *Für Elise* in front of her, hoping she'll play it well the first time through. Her body signals are going to tell you that the selection is too frustrating; she'll begin to fidget, tap her fingers, swing her feet, or cry. Why make her do something that blocks her progress and reinforces her dislike of reading?[3]

Your child's reading for *fun* selections should be on her Independent Level, and the *learning to read* selections must be on her Instructional Level.

Choosing Reading Selections

I was in the children's section of the library looking at books. I overheard a mom and her daughter in the next aisle:

"No, Charise. You can't have that book. It's too hard for you. Why don't you choose this book?" said Mom.

"But, I want that book. It's about sharks," said Charise.

"We can get that one later," said Mom. "Let's choose an easier book for you to read."

Did you hear what I heard? Charise actually chose a book! Then Mom made her put it back because she couldn't read it. *Hmmm.* Mom could have said, "That looks like a great book, Charise. Let's get it, and we'll get this book too."

When your child chooses a book, something about the book is calling to her. She has an interest in it. Run with this. She'll put effort into something she has chosen. When you grab your choices instead of hers, something in her dries up. Both of you can choose books for Practice Reading Time.

When I go to the library with a child, the first question I ask is "What do you like to read about?" Some children know right away. "I want to read about cheetahs or spaceships." Some children need to be paraded past a few aisles to see their choices.

Sometimes a child will choose a book with tiny print. No problem. With your help, she can read captions under the pictures. Or read most of the book to her and have her read a short paragraph per chapter. There's no textbook that says, "Your child must read the entire book by herself, or else. . . ."

Then I say to a child, "We're both going to choose some books. You choose (number) of books, and I'll choose (number) of books." This frees the child to choose whatever her heart desires. It also allows me to choose books on her Instructional level. I always try to choose books from topics that she likes.

Now take off your parent hat for a minute and put on a kid hat. Which would your child rather read—biographies of famous people or *Clifford* books? Don't get me wrong—lots of children like to read science experiment books or books about computers. But what books turn on a struggling reader? You need to get inside your child's head to find out.

Many children dislike reading so much that nothing interests them. Now what do you do? Every kid likes to laugh. Therefore, Dr. Seuss is a great favorite. If your child doesn't like him, there are joke books or silly poem books. Borrow these from the library to read with your child.

Often there is a chasm between what a child is willing to read and what her parent wants her to read. A child likes to read easy, familiar books because she feels successful. These selections are often at her Independent or Instructional Level. But a parent wants the child to read books at her grade level, which usually falls into her Frustration Level.

Mary Leonhardt, author of *Parents Who Love Reading, Kids Who Don't* says it isn't as important what your child reads, as long as she does lots of it.[4] If your child reads lots of easy books on her Independent

Level every day, her reading skills will improve. Sight words will become automatic. Your child will read more fluently. Soon she will get bored and choose more interesting selections.

Unfortunately, most struggling readers do little reading each day. It's a battle in which parents demand, threaten, or bribe their children to read. Parents often lose this battle, and their children lose the war. This is especially true of busy parents or children who are often home by themselves.

Here's how to win the battle. Put lots of your child's favorite books around her. Pay her to read books. Help her make her own books (see chapters 11 and 15), even if they are joke books. If your child spends time every day reading books, either with you or the babysitter, her skills will move forward. If she reads nothing in a day, nothing has been gained.

Getting Good Books

Many reluctant readers don't have books at home that they can successfully read. How can you find lots of easy-to-read books for children? There is a list of "leveled books" in appendix B. They are available at the public library or at your child's school library. Write down titles and ask the school librarian to send some home with your child.

Beg, borrow (but don't steal!) books from your friends and neighbors. Just as a child can't take flute lessons without having a flute, your child can't improve in reading skills unless she has lots of books.

Length of a Reading Selection: Reading to Excellence

When I was a child, my friend's dad made her sit down and read a half hour every day of the summer. But her reading sounded every bit as nonfluent on August 31 as it had in early June. I often wondered *Why didn't her reading improve?*

Her parents did well in making her read every day, but they didn't know that she should have been rereading short selections to excellence.[5] What does that mean?

Many children have never reread a short piece to excellence. They don't know that they *can* sound better when reading. This is similar to practicing the piano. The first time you play a piano selection, you'll play some wrong notes and your timing isn't quite right. You don't close the music book and say, "There, I'm done." You play the piece over and over. Harder sections are repeated, often one hand at a time, until they sound good. Then the whole piece is put together.

A short reading selection is *not* a whole book. It might be one or two very *easy* pages or a paragraph of four or five sentences. Here is an example of a short selection from *Thunderhoof,* by Syd Hoff (Harper & Row, 1971).

"Way out West, one great horse still ran wild. His name was Thunderhoof. Cowboys tried to catch him. But he ran too fast for them. If they got a rope around his neck, he shook it off. 'Nobody will ever catch me,' said Thunderhoof."

A short selection is too big to memorize, but not so big that it taxes short-term memory. Your child should reread it several times to make the selection sound good. This is far better than slugging through a whole book nonfluently.

Reading to excellence is the fluency goal for your child.

Fluency

Just as a rocket needs fuel to lift off, a child needs to read fluently in order to have comprehension. Remember that fluency is reading smoothly at a normal talking speed. Poor readers read in word fragments and each piece has no meaning: "I l-ike c-an-dy." Five pieces of that only yield a couple of words. Fluent readers read in chunks of

A short reading selection is not a whole book. It might be one or two very easy pages or a paragraph of four or five sentences.

words, such as in this example from *Dragon Gets By*, by Dav Pilkey (Orchard Books, 1991):

"When Dragon woke up — he was very groggy — and when he was groggy — he did everything wrong."

As you can see, more information can be remembered during fluent reading.

One of my professors had this opinion about nonfluent reading: Allowing a child to read nonfluently does more harm than good. It causes her to practice bad reading.[6] Was she suggesting that children not practice reading? Of course not! But she was countering nonfluent reading that occurs every night across America. Children butcher books while their moms wash dishes. The same professor went on to describe a technique that doesn't permit nonfluent reading, called *To, With, and By*.[7,8]

To, With, and By: *A Method to Improve Fluency*

The Air Force uses *To, With, and By* to train fighter pilots. It's called "Demonstration Performance Method" done by the Air Education and Training Command (AETC). Each training jet has two sets of flight controls, one for the teacher and one for the training pilot. The teacher shows a new maneuver *to* the training pilot by demonstrating it. Then the teacher does the new maneuver together *with* the training pilot a few times, and finally the pilot does it *by* himself.

Since the Air Force uses *To, With, and By* to teach young pilots, you can bet it's a good method because they are working with multi-million dollar aircraft. For your child, learning to read is much more important than learning how to fly.

To, With, and By has been used by other tutors, including me, to catapult hundreds of children into fluent reading. Doing *To, With, and By* is as easy as 1-2-3.

Choose a short selection on your child's Instructional Reading Level. (Remember the 1:20 readability rule: no more than one or two mistakes per twenty words.) Then do the following.

To

"Tassie," said Mom, "I am going to read this *to* you two times. I want you to listen, and look at the words with your eyes."

- Make sure your child doesn't say anything during this time; she is supposed to be listening.
- Read at a natural speed, running your finger under the words. Your child should be looking at words in the book, not at your mouth.
- Read the same sentences again *to* her. If you read too slowly, you'll lose your child's attention. Her attention might drift to watching a spider crawl up the wall instead.

With

"Tassie, I want you to read this *with* me now," said Mom.

- Read the same sentences *with* your child, twice.
- Make sure she's not mumbling. However, she probably won't be saying every word with you either.
- Don't slow down when she reads with you. The selection is now becoming familiar to your child.

By

"Okay, Tassie," said Mom. "Read this *by* yourself."

- Help her fix a miscalled word (see chapter 5 for fixing mistakes). She should reread the sentence, putting the word in correctly.
- Have her read the selection twice *by herself*. Her reading will sound far better than had she "sounded it out" word by word.

Your child will expect that all reading should sound fluent. It will help her learn sight words, increase fluency, and improve her comprehension skills. She will gain confidence and experience instant success in reading. Best of all, *To, With, and By* positively affects your child's future attempts to read.

Ballet is also taught using *To, With, and By*. A dance teacher demonstrates some new steps in front of her student. The student imitates the teacher while they dance the number together. Finally the student performs them by herself, with the teacher's encouragement. This is practiced over and over until it looks effortless.

You might be thinking, "My kid has to learn to read herself. I can't hold her hand." Remember the best form of teaching is *modeling*. This is exactly what *To, With, and By* does—it models good reading.

I can almost hear you say, "But she isn't getting enough practice if she isn't reading the whole book. How can this help her?" My answer is, "A little bit of excellent reading is far better than a whole lot of bad reading."

To, With, and By gets as great results in reading as it does in flying and dancing. If you do this one technique, ignoring the rest of this book, you will make a positive difference in your child's ability to read. Be sure to do *To, With, and By* at least twice with your child every time you read together.

Alternating Reading

Let's say that you've done *To, With, and By*, and you want to finish the book. You can finish the book during fun reading time, or use another reading technique: read it alternately.

Alternating reading is when you read a paragraph out loud and your child reads the next paragraph. Or take turns reading pages. Kids love to read shorter pages, letting you read the longer pages. Run your finger under the words to keep her attention while you are reading.

Remember the best form of teaching is modeling, *which is exactly what* To, With, and By *does.*

Alternating reading helps your child's comprehension, and it keeps her involved while the book is being read.

Alternating reading helps your child's comprehension, and it keeps her involved while the book is being read.

In reading a book with a child, I begin by reading two pages to her. We do a paragraph using *To, With, and By.* She reads a (very) short page to me. I read a couple of pages to her. Then we do another *To, With, and By* segment. I read a couple more pages, and pretty soon we have finished the book.

If your child has a science or history homework assignment that falls in her Frustration Reading Level, take turns reading it and do two segments of *To, With, and By.* Your child might discover that she likes history after all!

To, With, and By and alternating reading will help empower your child in reading. Your child will read more fluently; she will memorize vocabulary words in a painless way; and she will gain the attitude, "I can do this."

Information to Remember

○ Help your child read selections on her Instructional Reading Level.

○ A reading selection should be one or two *easy* pages or a paragraph (three to four sentences long).

○ Use *To, With, and By* on short selections to help your child read fluently.

○ Read alternately with your child to finish a book or complete homework assignments.

CHAPTER 5

Let's Fix It!

Dealing with Reading Mistakes

Abe read to his Mom. She absentmindedly listened to him while making supper:

"Ouch!" said Sam. "Something bit me."
"Ouch!" said Jan. "Something bit me too."
"It's a bunch of mokipples!" yelled Sam.
"They jumped up and down and ran around."
—from *There Is a Carrot in My Ear and Other Noodle Tales*,
by Alvin Schwartz, HarperTrophy, 1982

The selection replayed itself in Mom's ear. "It's a bunch of *what*?" she asked.

Abe said, "A bunch of mokipples."

"What on earth is a *mokipple*?" asked Mom.

Abe said, "I don't know."

Mom sat down beside him and said, "I hope I don't bump into any *mokipples* when we go camping, Abe. Let's fix that word because it needs to make sense."

It's a temptation to correct every mistake that a child makes. But too many interruptions affect a child's fluency and comprehension. Don't forget, comprehension is the ultimate goal in reading. So choose your battles, and help your child fix mistakes that affect his reading the most.

Good and Bad Reading Mistakes

All reading mistakes are not equal. If your child misreads a word and it makes sense, it's a *good* mistake. Don't interrupt his reading to fix it.[1]

If your child misreads a word and it doesn't make sense, this is a *bad* mistake that must be fixed because it is destroying comprehension. Here are examples of both mistakes:

Good Mistakes

"The cow *hopped* (jumped) over the moon."

"She climbed the *mountain* (hill) to see the sunset."

"This is the *store* (shop)."

Bad Mistakes

"The cow *jilled* (jumped) over the moon."

"She climbed the *hungry* (hill) to see the sunset."

"This is the *sheggle* (shop)."

Sometimes good mistakes have few (if any) letters in common with the original word. But good mistakes have similar meanings to the original word. Someday, when your child reads a lot better, he can fix good mistakes.

Bad mistakes are invented words not found in the English language. Or they don't make sense in the sentence. It's a problem when your child makes bad mistakes and continues reading as if nothing has happened. He needs to self-monitor what he's reading, to ensure that it makes sense.

Your child is improving when he says a bad mistake and pauses. He looks at the word more closely and tries reading it again. He has learned that the purpose of reading is to make sense.

All reading mistakes are not equal. If your child misreads a word and it makes sense, it's a good mistake. Don't interrupt his reading to fix it.

> *Believe that your child is doing the best he can on his first try. If he reads a word incorrectly, he doesn't know it.*

Fixing Reading Mistakes

Here's an example of how *not* to fix a child's reading mistake. David is reading about a farmer:

Mom said, "Honey, that word is *fence*."

He made the same mistake again.

Mom said, "David, you know that word. Now, read it right."

David got frustrated and started to cry.

Mom yelled, "This is easy. Why can't you remember this?"

Have you ever done this? If you want Practice Reading Time to be a positive experience for both of you, something else will have to happen.

Believe that your child is doing the best he can on his first try. If he reads a word incorrectly, he doesn't know it. Saying, "I know you know this. You've read it before," or "Just sound it out," will not magically help him read the word. Don't let your child hesitate for more than two seconds without helping him. Long hesitations destroy fluency—and nonfluency is the enemy of reading.

Strategies for Fixing a Reading Mistake

Give your child a strategy to fix mistakes, and you've given him a gift. Helping him practice the strategy is like unwrapping the gift. Here are some strategies:

- Let him finish the sentence and say, "Did that make sense? Let's go back and fix it."

- Tell him, "Look at the *first two letters* and get your mouth ready to say the sound." If the remaining letters in the word distract him, teach him to finger block—by covering them with his finger.

Here is *your* strategy when he hesitates on a long word: Say the word in *two or three parts* and have him put it together. Then ask him to reread the sentence. (For more about this strategy, see "Put the Word Together Game" on page 117.)

Alan says, "They came to race from o-t-t"

"That word is ou-t-er," says Mom.

"Outer space," says Alan.

"Now put it in the sentence," says Mom.

Alan says, "They came to race from outer space." (From *Space Race* by Judith Stamper, Scholastic, 1998.)

"Good job," says Mom.

Above all, don't allow him to sit there looking at the word—that destroys fluency. Either *he* has to use a strategy or *you* need to intervene.

Reread the Sentence

"Calen, when you make a mistake, we'll fix the word. Then you're going to reread the sentence saying it correctly," said Dad.

"I don't want to read it again," said Calen.

"I know," said Dad, "but you want to become a good reader, right? That's what good readers do—they fix a word and reread the sentence. Pretty soon all your words will be correct."

"Okay," said Calen as he picked up *S-S-Snakes!* and began to read.

After your child has fixed a word, make him reread the sentence. *This is the most important part of fixing a mistake.* When he rereads the sentence, his brain is learning the word. Next time your child sees that word, he has a better chance of recognizing it.

Let's look at several examples from a selection to see how to fix mistakes. Here's one from *Cat Traps* by Molly Coxe (Random House, 1996):

When your child rereads a sentence, his brain is learning the word. Next time he sees that word, he has a better chance of recognizing it.

Cat wants a snack. Cat sets a trap. Cat gets a bug. Ugh!

Cat wants a snack. Cat sets a trap. Cat gets a pig. Too big!

Cat wants a snack. Cat sets a trap. Cat gets a fish. Swish!

Example #1   Child says: "Cat *wents* a snack."

Dad says: "Did that make sense?"

Child: "No."

Dad: "What didn't make sense?"

Child: "Wents."

Dad: "That's right. That word is w-a-nts."

Child: "Wants."

Dad: "Good job. Now read that sentence again."

Child: "Cat wants a snack."

Example #2   Child says: "Cat wants a snack. Cat makes a trap. Cat gets a bug. Ugh!"

(Since "makes" is similar to "sets" in meaning, Dad doesn't fix the word. He lets his child continue reading.)

Example #3   Child says: "Cat wants a snack. Cat sets a trap. Cat gets a . . ."

Dad says: "Look at the first two letters, and get your mouth ready to say their sound. What do they say?"

Child: "pi . . . oh, pig."

Dad: "That's right. The word is pig. Now please read that sentence again."

Child: "Cat sets a trap. Cat gets a pig. Too big."

Dad: "That sounded good!"

Example #4   Child says: "Cat wants a snack. Cat sets a trap. Cat gets a *frish swallow*."

Dad says: "Did that make sense?"

Child: "No."

Dad: "What didn't make sense?"

Child: "Frish swallow."

Dad: "Good. The word is f-i-sh."

Child: "Fish. Cat gets a fish. Sw . . ."
Dad: "That word rhymes with fish."
Child: "Swish."
Dad: "Okay, now read the whole sentence."
Child: "Cat wants a snack. Cat sets a trap. Cat gets a fish. Swish."
Dad: "Good Job."

Information to Remember

○ Good mistakes that make sense don't need to be fixed.

○ Help your child to figure out unknown words using these strategies:

> Look at the first two letters, and get your mouth ready to say the sound.

> Make it make sense.

○ Don't let your child hesitate more than two seconds on an unknown word.

○ Give it to him in two or three parts, to put together and say it correctly.

○ Always make him reread the sentence with the corrected word.

CHAPTER 6

What Level?

Testing Your Child

Children fall into one of three broad reading levels *based not on their age or their grade in school* but on the reading skills they have or don't have. We don't worry about four year olds who can't remember alphabet letters. However, six year olds should know letters *and* sounds. This is also true about rhyming and reading simple sentences.

Let's give your child a quick test. Depending on the results of the test, you will begin rescue reading on Level 1, Level 2, or Level 3. The test has three parts:

1. Rhyming

2. Identifying alphabet letters and saying letter sounds

3. Reading a short story

Find a quiet place in your house and give this test when your child is well rested. The test should take no more than ten minutes. When she's done, praise your child for her efforts because this is hard work for her.

Photocopy the Student Test Sheet (on page 46) and your Answer Sheet (on page 43) in case you want to give this test again someday. A retest will indicate your child's improvement in reading skills.

Directions for Test

- Sit together at a table or sit slightly behind your child. She will feel less nervous if she can't see your notes on the Answer Sheet.

- Give her the *Student Test Sheet* (photocopy it or carefully tear it out of this book).

- Mark her answers on your *Answer Sheet*.

- Ask her to give the best answers she can. If she hesitates, mark the answer wrong. If she quickly corrects herself, mark it correct. (Quick answers show good recall of the information.)

- Write down exactly what your child says to catch the nature of her mistakes. (Incorrect responses show that she doesn't understand rhyming or is having letter confusion. For example, if she sees a *b* and says *d* sound, she's mixing those letters in her mind.)

- Don't help your child, even if you are "sure" she knows an answer. You need to know how she does on her own.

- Ask your child to run her finger under letters or words, so you know where she is.

Answer Sheet for Student Test Sheet (page 46)

—photocopy if you want to retest later

Rhyming Test

Say: "I am going to say a word, and I want you to say a word that rhymes with it. For example, if I say 'house' you might say 'mouse.'"

Ask your child to say a word that rhymes with each of these words.

cat _____ bed _____ pig _____

hot _____ bug _____ crash _____

Were her answers automatic? Yes ___✓___ No _____

Letter Name Test

Ask your child to name the letters. Write any incorrect answers beside the letters.

p ____ m ____ s ____ c *l* i ____ x *l*

l ____ e ____ w ____ d ____ j ____ z ____

n ____ b ____ u ____ k ____ g ____ f ____

o ____ r ____ t ____ y ____ a ____ v ____

h ____ q ____

Letter Sound Test—*Use the same set of alphabet letters.*

Ask your child to tell you what each letter "says." (I have included words to help you identify the correct *sound*.)

Check incorrect sounds and write your child's answers beneath the letters.

p (pizza) ☐　　**m** (mouse) ☐　　**s** (snake) ☐　　　**c** (cake) ☐　　**i** (igloo) ☐　　**x** (axe) ☐

l (lion) ☐　　　**e** (elephant) ☐　**w** (walrus) ☐　　**d** (dog) ☐　　**j** (jet) ☐　　**z** (zebra) ☐

n (nest) ☐　　　**b** (boat) ☐　　**u** (umbrella) ☐　**k** (kite) ☐　　**g** (gift) ☐　　**f** (fish) ☐

o (octopus) ☐　**r** (rabbit) ☐　　**t** (turtle) ☐　　　**y** (yo-yo) ☐　**a** (apple) ☐　**v** (violin) ☐

h (hat) ☐　　　**q** (*q* says "qw" as in queen because *q* is always followed by *u* in the English language) ☐

Read the Story Test

Ask your child to read Story #1 (p. 46). Tell her to do the best she can.

Circle and write down mistakes—words that were omitted, read incorrectly, or took longer than four seconds to read. (Count seconds as one thousand one, one thousand two . . .)

Story #1: The Cat
Jim has a cat. His cat went up a tree. Will the cat get down? Mom will help the cat. Now Jim has his cat back.

Number of Reading Mistakes ____

Was your child's reading fluent? Yes ☐   No ☐

If she makes three or more mistakes on Story #1, The Cat, the test is finished.

If she makes fewer than three mistakes, ask her to read Story #2, The Hamster (page 46).

Story #2: My Hamster
I have a pet hamster. Once a week I clean his cage. Every day I give him some food and fill his bottle with water. My hamster wakes up at night. He runs in his wheel and eats his food. He is a good pet.

Number of Reading Mistakes ____

Was your child's reading fluent? Yes ☐   No ☐

Student Test Sheet—*give this sheet to your student*

Alphabet Letters and Sounds

p	m	s	c	i	x
l	e	w	d	j	z
n	b	u	k	g	f
o	r	t	y	a	v
h	q				

The Cat

Jim has a cat. His cat went up a tree. Will the cat get down? Mom will help the cat. Now Jim has his cat back.

My Hamster

I have a pet hamster. Once a week I clean his cage. Every day I give him some food and fill his bottle with water. My hamster wakes up at night. He runs in his wheel and eats his food. He is a good pet.

Determine Your Child's Rescue Reading Level

Results of Letter Names and Letter Sounds Tests

What letters or letter sounds did your child miss (see your answers on pages 43 and 44)? Write them below.

Letter Names: Letter Sounds:

Do you see any patterns in the errors?

- Do consonant letters that your child missed look similar? (For example, p/q/g, or i/l/j, or m/n/w, d/b, or u/v.)

- Did she miss most of the vowels?

- Did she add a pronounced "uh" to the sounds of many of the letters?

Based on information from pages 43 and 44, answer these questions:

Does your child know how to rhyme?	Yes ☐	No ☐
Does your child know the names of the entire alphabet?	Yes ☐	No ☐
Does your child know the *sounds* of the entire alphabet?	Yes ☐	No ☐
Did your child make fewer than three mistakes on Story #1?	Yes ☐	No ☐
Did your child sound fluent while reading Story #1?	Yes ☐	No ☐
Did your child make fewer than three mistakes on Story #2?	Yes ☐	No ☐
Did your child sound fluent while reading Story #2?	Yes ☐	No ☐

If you begin at too high a reading level, both you and your child will be frustrated because there won't be a foundation of skills to build upon.

Let's match the test results to the Rescue Reading Level. (Check all that apply to your child.)

Level 1 Reader

☐ Is unable to rhyme

☐ Doesn't know all the names of the alphabet

☐ Doesn't know all the sounds of the alphabet

☐ Made three or more mistakes on Story #1

Level 2 Reader

☐ Knows how to rhyme

☐ Knows all the names of the alphabet

☐ Knows all the sounds of the alphabet, but needs review of short vowel sounds

☐ Made fewer than three mistakes on Story #1, but more than three mistakes on Story #2

Level 3 Reader

☐ Knows how to rhyme

☐ Knows the names of the alphabet

☐ Knows all the sounds of the alphabet

☐ Made less than three mistakes on Story #1 and Story #2

☐ Sounds nonfluent while reading Story #2

Choose a Rescue Reading level based on the objective results of this test—not on what you "think" your child knows. Some children straddle two levels. If that's true with your child, choose the lower level. She will probably complete it quickly. If you begin at too high a level, both you and your child will be frustrated because there won't be a foundation of skills to build upon.

It's not uncommon to have a ten-year-old begin on Level 1. The information is user-friendly for both older and younger children. Get yourself a cup of tea, some paper and a pencil, and begin teaching your child reading skills to last a lifetime.

Information to Remember

○ Photocopy the test and your answer pages (before using them). This way you can give a retest.

○ Determine on which level your child should begin working, based on results from the test.

○ Choose a level based on your child's reading skills, not on age or grade in school.

© EYEWIRE

PART II

*Rescuing a Level 1
Reader*

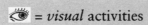 = *visual* activities

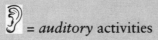 = *auditory* activities

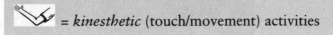 = *kinesthetic* (touch/movement) activities

Portrait of a Level 1 Reader

Danny always had a smile and especially liked to play Nintendo. Halfway through first grade he could read his name and the word "the." His two-word vocabulary didn't bother him at all.

Danny's parents, busy with three kids and two jobs, didn't realize anything was amiss. They thought Danny, who seemed as smart as his older brother, would easily learn to read. Besides, his grades were good. When Danny's teacher expressed her concerns at a parent-teacher conference, his parents were surprised.

In testing Danny, I discovered that he recognized alphabet letters and knew some consonant sounds. He put word parts together to say words. *So far, so good,* I thought.

But Danny was unable to rhyme, didn't know vowel sounds, and couldn't read any words on a page. His writing skills consisted of writing his first name. When I told him a simple three-part story (in three sentences), he was unable to retell it.

During tutoring sessions we worked on rhyming skills. He learned short vowel sounds and began to read three-letter words. We created books, and read predictable books.

Danny's parents were part of his reading team. I taught them how to do *To, With, and By.* They helped him practice rhyming and making words from letter squares. Danny read lots of homemade and predictable books. He's going to be rescued from a lifetime of illiteracy.

CHAPTER 7

Half Hour to *Hop on Pop*

Daily Schedule for Beginners

My brothers read a little bit.
Little words like *if* and *it*.
My father can read big words, too.
Like *Constantinople* and *Timbuktu*.
—from *Hop on Pop* by Dr. Seuss, Random House, 1963

Lots of skills occur between reading words *if* and *Timbuktu*. Parents often choose selections for their child based on his age, or what his peers are reading at school. By doing this, the child's gaps don't get filled and he continues to read nonfluently. It's like driving a Mercedes on a road with big potholes. The ride doesn't become smooth until the potholes are properly filled in—and we know that reading should sound smooth.

Daily Schedule for Working on Reading Skills

Kyle knows the alphabet letters except *q* and *p,* which he mixes up. He also knows most of the consonant sounds, but confuses the vowel sounds. He can read the first five pages of *Hop on Pop* by himself. Kyle is well on his way to understanding the "Alphabetic

> *The "Alphabetic Principle" is the idea that alphabet letters represent the sounds we hear in words.*

Principle"—the idea that alphabet letters represent the sounds we hear in words.

Joseph knows the letter *J*, which begins his name, and the letter *s* for stop sign. You can see that Joseph, who is at the beginning of letter/sound knowledge, is in a different place conceptually than Kyle.

Level 1 is divided into three stages to accommodate differences children like Joseph and Kyle have in letter/sound knowledge. (Activities for each of the three stages are presented in greater detail in chapters 8–11.)

Stage A is for the child who *needs to learn most* of the alphabet letters and sounds. You might wonder, "At this beginning stage, what materials are easy enough for him to read?" He will read an alphabet book he has created and stories that he dictates to you—they will be quickly memorized. Here is the schedule for Stage A children:

Stage A: Daily Half-Hour Schedule

5 minutes	Create an alphabet book	(see chapter 8)
5 minutes	Teach how to rhyme	(see chapter 9)
5 minutes	Make a book	(see chapter 11)
15 minutes	Practice Reading Time— have him read his homemade books out loud	(see chapter 4)

Stage B is for the child who *knows most* of the alphabet letters and sounds, but still has a few more to learn. Here is the schedule for Stage B children:

Stage B: Daily Half-Hour Schedule		
5 minutes	Learn letter sounds using the Alphabet Chart	(see chapter 8)
5 minutes	Teach how to rhyme	(see chapter 9)
5 minutes	Make a book	(see chapter 11)
15 minutes	Practice Reading Time—have him read his homemade books out loud, and predictable books using the *To, With, and By* technique	(see chapter 4)

Stage C is for the child who *knows all* of the alphabet letters and sounds. He is ready to put three letters (consonant-vowel-consonant) together to make words. Your child will feel proud as he applies his knowledge of letter sounds to making and reading words. Here is the schedule for Stage C children:

Stage C: Daily Half-Hour Schedule		
5 minutes	Put letters together to make words	(see chapter 10)
5 minutes	Teach how to rhyme and play games for auditory memory	(see chapter 9)
5 minutes	Make a book	(see chapter 11)
15 minutes	Practice Reading Time—have him read his homemade books out loud, and predictable books using the *To, With, and By* technique	(see chapter 4)

Joseph will be doing different things in Stage A than Kyle in Stage B. Joseph will be making an alphabet book and looking at alphabet books from the library. Kyle will be learning a few letters and sounds from an alphabet chart. He will also be reading predictable books.

These are books with lots of repeated segments—either in sentences or phrases. Children of all ages are thrilled to be able to "read" a predictable book after hearing it read a couple of times.

In Stage C, both Joseph and Kyle will be putting alphabet letter squares (see figure 10.1 on page 84) together to read easy words, and playing games to strengthen their auditory memories. It may be possible for Joseph to jump over Stage B and go right into Stage C.

Based on results from the alphabet letter names and sounds test (see previous chapter), decide which stage is most appropriate to begin with your child. Don't forget: every Level 1 Reader needs to complete Stage C to become a Level 2 Reader.

You may be thinking, "Hey, my child is ten years old. He's too old for this!" I have found that older children enjoy playing these games, and making their own books. They will move through this level quickly.

Photocopy Today's Work Sheet: Level 1 Reader (see page 58), making enough copies for the next several weeks. This sheet will help organize each day's half-hour reading time together. Keep your materials together in a box or drawer—ready for the next day. Also, keep the pace up, and don't let it drag. There's always tomorrow to finish something that was started today.

By going through Stages A, B, and C, your child's reading skills will get stronger. All of a sudden you'll realize he is ready to read selections from more challenging books. Your hard work together will pay off. He'll be ready to begin as a Level 2 Reader!

Level 1 Reader

Children of all ages are thrilled to be able to "read" a predictable book after hearing it read a couple of times.

Today's Worksheet

Level 1 Reader

Child's Name: Date:

[5 minutes]   **Teach Alphabet Letters and Sounds (see chapter 8).**
Work on homemade alphabet book ☐ or

Use Alphabet Letter Chart ☐ or

Put letters together to make words (see chapter 10)

Alphabet letter/sound we are learning today:
Letter/sounds to review:

_____   _____   _____

_____   _____   _____

[5 minutes]   **Teach How to Rhyme (see chapter 9)**
Do rhyming sheet on page:
Read rhyming book: (write down title) _____
Play game to strengthen auditory memory (see page 79):
(write down game) _____

[5 minutes]   **The book we made today is (see chapter 11)**
(write down title) _____

[15 minutes]   **Practice Reading Time**
Read alphabet book (write down title) _____

Read homemade book: (write down title) _____

Read predictable book (see chapter 11):
(write down title) _____

Comments:

Information to Remember

○ Begin working in Stage A, B, or C, whichever best fits your child's needs. This is based on the results of testing your child from chapter 6.

○ Work together for a half hour each day.

○ When your child is successful at one stage, move to the next higher one.

○ When he has completed Stage C, he is ready to be a Level 2 Reader.

Level 1 Reader

CHAPTER 8

Apples to Zebras

Teach the Alphabet

There's a story about a prince who wrote a letter on his first day at school. The proud king went to tell the queen, who told her mother, who told the maid, and so on. Each person embellished the story so that in a short time, two kingdoms were ready for war because of the letter the prince wrote. Finally, the son of the castle cook said,

"Please, tell me what you wrote."

"Well," said Prince Paul proudly. "Yesterday I wrote a letter 'a'. And today I am going to learn how to write a letter 'b'."

— from *The Prince Who Wrote a Letter*, by Ann Love, Scholastic, 1992.

Knowing the letters of the alphabet won't usually cause a war. But, not knowing alphabet letter names and sounds can cause illiteracy. The foundation for reading is instantaneous knowledge of alphabet sounds.

You may have thought that your child knew the alphabet because she watched *Sesame Street* a million times or she's in school. But now you know (through testing results) that she has gaps in her alphabet letter/sound knowledge.

The real question is "What does she know automatically?" It is one thing for her to spend time thinking and come up with an answer. But to be able to read, she must be able to give instant answers to such questions as the following:

Parent: "What does letter *a* say?"
Child: "*A* says *aah* for apple."

Notice that an alphabet letter and its sound are taught together. Children with automatic knowledge of letter sounds have a solid foundation for reading new words.

Level 1 Reader

Notice that an alphabet letter and its sound are taught together. Children with automatic knowledge of letter *sounds* have a solid foundation for reading new words. Children who don't have next to nothing to build on.

Some letters have more than one sound. Say the following words, and listen to the different sounds that letter *a* makes: *apple, above, any, almost, navy*. It's not necessary to teach every sound that letter *a* makes—they will be learned as your child reads connected print. For now, teach your child the most common sound a letter makes by using the Alphabet Chart (see figure 8.1).

Teach your child the "short" vowel (a, e, i, o, u) sounds first. Later, it will be easy to say, "Try the other sound, which is its name."

When you are teaching letter sounds, be careful not to add an "uh" sound at the end of a letter. Letter s says "sss," not "suh." It should sound like a hissing snake, with no throat sound. If your child learns letters *c, a, t* as sounding "kuh," "aah," and "tuh," those sounds will not come together to say cat! As much as possible, try not to add that awful "uh" sound.

Stage A: Teach Her Name and Create Your Own Alphabet Book

A quick jump-start for a child is to teach her the letters in her name. She will be highly motivated to learn them.

The next step is to create an alphabet book (see figure 8.2). When your child *chooses* items and draws pictures of them, she will learn alphabet letters more easily. For modeling purposes, you'll write in the alphabet book. Invite your child to trace the letters with different colored markers.

Figure 8.1

The Alphabet Chart

A a B b C c D d

E e F f G g H h

I i J j K k L l

M m N n O o P p

Q q R r S s T t

U u V v W w X x

Y y Z z

> *A quick jump-start for a child is to teach her the letters in her name.*

1. Fold a stack of seven pieces of paper in half and staple the edge.
2. On the front, write "(your child's name)'s Alphabet Book."
3. On the inside page, write capital *A* and small *a*—both in large print. Ask your child to draw an *ant* on that page. Let her choose other letter *a* words to illustrate.

Be sure to use items that contain short vowel sounds. For example:

- Aa—ant, apple, alligator, acrobat
- Ee—elephant, egg, enchilada
- Ii—iguana, Indian, igloo
- Oo—octopus, otter, ostrich
- Uu—buffalo, umbrella, umpire

Teach the letters *Cc* and *Gg* "hard" sound first.

- Cc—camel, cat, candy, cup
- Gg—goose, gorilla, girl, grandmother

Look at the Alphabet Chart to get ideas for other letters.

Go at a pace that allows your child to really learn the letters. It's better to teach one letter at a time. Add new letters only after you are sure she has learned the previous letters. Each day ask your child to read her alphabet book to you. She should point to the letters and say:

Letter name	sound	word
A	*aah*	ant
B	*b*	boat
C	*k*	camel
D	*d*	dog

Figure 8.2 Shelby's Alphabet Book

It's important that your child says the letter name first, then the sound of the letter, and the picture name. If she reads her alphabet book to you every day, she will know it backwards and forwards.

Sing the Alphabet Song

Just about every child in America has sung the ABCD alphabet song to the tune of *Twinkle Twinkle Little Star*, which ends with "Next time won't you sing with me?" Don't assume that your child already knows this song. You are going to have to find out by asking her to sing it to you.

Learning facts by singing accesses a different part of the brain than talking does. (One surgeon stuttered so badly when he talked that he sang his directions to the nurses!) Don't worry if you have a frog in your throat.

The alphabet song can be sung in lots of ways: pretend to be a bear and sing it in a gruff voice, or a mouse with a squeaky voice. I sang it many times in the car with my captive audience listening. Even if your child doesn't join by singing, she will learn it simply by listening.

After hearing the alphabet song, one child asked her Mom, "What's an 'el-em-en-no-pee?'" To avoid auditory confusion, point to letters on the Alphabet Chart as you are singing the alphabet song.

Learning facts by singing accesses a different part of the brain than talking does.

Look at Alphabet Books

The library has lots of alphabet books. One type has one letter per page with pictures. For example, letter *c* page might have a cricket, crow, and castle. Children make connections between letters and the beginning sounds of the items. A good example is *Animals A to Z* by David McPhail, Scholastic, 1989.

Another type of alphabet book is *Animalia* by Graeme Base (Abrams, 1986). Each page has a picture and a sentence such as "Great green gorillas growing grapes in a gorgeous glass greenhouse." Doesn't that sound rich rolling off your tongue?

Here are other alphabet books to check out at your local library.

Alphabet City by Stephen T. Johnson, Viking, 1995. Alphabet letters are cleverly found in different parts of a city.

Clifford's ABC by Norman Bridwell, Scholastic, 1983. Clifford has friends and objects that begin with each alphabet letter.

A Is for Angry: an Animal and Adjective Alphabet by Sandra Boynton, Workman Publishing, 1987. Pages illustrate a short phrase, such as "I is for ill," with an ill iguana.

The Yucky Reptile Alphabet Book by Jerry Pallota, Charlesbridge Publishing, 1989. There is a picture and description of a reptile for each letter of the alphabet. (Jerry Pallota has created an entire series of alphabet books.)

Trace Alphabet Letters

"Mandy, watch me write the letter *c*," said Dad. He pointed the pencil on a piece of paper. "It starts at 2 o'clock and goes down around. Can you trace my letter *c*?"

Modeling is the best form of teaching. Take two minutes each night to model how to write a letter. Then let your child trace it with colored markers, making rainbow letters.

Children often don't like to write because they don't know how to form letters. They haven't had enough practice for letters to be automatic. Look at the Writing Chart of lower case letters (see figure 8.3).

Notice that *all* printed letters start up and *go down*.

A big mistake children make in writing is that they start on the bottom line and go up. The letters don't look right and these children have a difficult time reading their own print. A few minutes of practice each night makes all the difference for them.

Stage B: Teach Specific Letters Using the Alphabet Chart

"Dana, listen to these words," said Mom. "Goose, gift, glee, giggle. What sound do you hear in each of those words?"

Figure 8.3 Writing chart of lower case letters

"I hear the 'g' sound," said Dana.

"That's right. Letter *g* says 'g' as in goose," said Mom. "Do you know what a goose is?"

"A goose is a big bird," said Dana.

"Yes," said Mom. "Remember when we went to the park and saw a Canadian goose sleeping? It was brown with a white tummy and a black neck."

"And it woke up and ate our bread crumbs," said Dana.

"That's right. Now look at the alphabet chart. This is letter *g*," Mom said, pointing to the letter. "Look at letter *g*, then close your eyes. I want you to make a picture of a goose in your head, and put a big letter *g* beside it. Do you see it?"

"Yes," said Dana with her eyes shut.

"Okay, what does letter *g* say?" said Mom.

"*G* says 'g' as in goose," said Dana.

Mom said, "Can you think of any other words that begin with the 'g' sound?"

Dana said, "How about *game* and *gorilla?*"

"Good job!" said Mom.

Get the Alphabet Chart (see figure 8.1) and sit beside your child. Ask her to watch your mouth when you make a letter sound. Help her to analyze how your mouth makes the sound. Is your tongue involved? Is your throat making noise? Then ask her to make the same sound and point to the alphabet letter.

You are the one who must teach your child this information. You can't hand your child an alphabet book or alphabet chart and say, "Here, learn it." It takes direct instruction on your part. *This is especially true for a child who has graduated from kindergarten without having learned the letter sounds.*

Children have different learning rates. Don't become discouraged if this process takes time. Your child may need lots of direct instruction to learn alphabet letter sounds to an automatic level. Don't forget she will learn letter sounds more quickly with a short daily review.

> You can't hand your child an alphabet book or alphabet chart and say, "Here, learn it." It takes direct instruction on your part.

Alphabet Games to Play

Games are a wonderful way to promote "automaticity"—which means your child sees it and says it right away. Even the most reluctant learner can be motivated by a game. Play some of these games for a few minutes and stop while your child is having a good time. She'll want to play again tomorrow.

Say the Name Game

This game will help your child identify alphabet letters. When she is able to identify most of the letters from the chart, write the alphabet letters on squares of paper.

How to Play

- Put the squares into a sock.
- Take turns pulling a square out and saying the name of the letter. (Keep the alphabet chart nearby for reference.)
- If the name is incorrect the square goes back into the sock.
- Whoever has the most squares wins.

To play another game, have your child pull letters out of the sock and arrange them in alphabetical order on the floor or a table. Some children sing the alphabet song while doing this activity.

Say the Sound Game

This game will help your child practice letter sounds.

How to Play

- Point to a letter on the Alphabet Chart.

- Ask your child to say its *sound*.

- When she knows most of the sounds, then do the opposite; you say a letter *sound*, then your child points to the letter.

If you want to make this game harder, ask your child to close her eyes. Say a letter sound, then have her open her eyes and point to the letter on the chart.

Silly Sentence Game

This game will give your child more practice with a specific letter sound.

How to Play

- This game begins when you say, "Anytime I say a word with a *p* (or other) sound in it, I want you to raise your hand."

- Say a sentence that has at least one word containing the *p* sound. You can have fun thinking of silly sentences with lots of *p*'s such as: "The purple penguin placed a pickle on his picnic table."

- Or, read a selection from a book with a lot of *p*'s in it. Your child will enjoy raising her hand a bunch of times.

- Or, have your child say the sentences and you raise your hand. She will enjoy creating sentences and making Mom raise her hand too!

Apply Letter Sounds to Connected Print

We don't want knowledge of letters and sounds to sit in a compartment in your child's brain unused. So connect letters to connected print:

How to Play

- Open your child's favorite book and ask her to point to specific alphabet letters on a page.

- Read words to her containing that letter.
- Ask her to read the words.

This is somewhat complicated by letters that make more than one sound, such as short and long vowels. Just tell her: "Sometimes this letter makes another sound. You will learn the other sound later."

When your child has learned alphabet letters and sounds you can put the alphabet books and chart away—unless of course, she is teaching them to her little brother.

Information to Remember

- Teach your child letter names and sounds she does not yet know.
- Be careful not to add an "uh" sound to the end of letter sounds.
- Play games to help your child learn the letter sounds to an automatic level.

CHAPTER 9

Rhyme Time

Helping Ears to Hear and the Brain to Remember

One day I asked Keith, "Tell me something that rhymes with dog." He said, "Dolphin." *Hmm,* I thought. He thinks that rhyming is alliteration—saying things that begin with the same letter such as *dog discovers a dirty diaper.* I knew Keith's parents read Dr. Seuss books to him, but up to now, no one thought to check whether he could rhyme.

Rhyming is done with the ears. It's an important part of phonological awareness—the ability to hear sounds within language. It precedes reading word families such as *cat, bat, chat,* and *splat.* Rhyming helps children manipulate words by taking them apart and inserting new beginnings.

"Sherry," said Dad, "Take the word *far* and remove the *f.* What do you have?"

"Ar."

"That's right. Now add a *st* in front. What do you have?"

"Star."

"Take the *st* away and add a *c* in front. What do you have?"

"Car."

"Good job! Can you think of any more *ar* words?"

Sherry and her dad are playing a rhyming game that can be played anywhere. Rhyming is fun and educational at the same time.

Some words rhyme but the endings don't look the same: *flour, power,* or *past, gassed.* It doesn't matter how they look—if they sound the same, they rhyme.

Rhyming is done through the ears and not the eyes.

Here are three activity pages to help teach rhyming to your child. You will notice that rhyming sounds are introduced to your child's ears first, because rhyming is done through his ears and not his eyes. Read and reread the sheets. Books written in rhymes are suggested to put rhyming into connected print.

Do five minutes of rhyming practice per day and remember:

A rhyme a day will succeed
in helping your child learn to read

Rhyme Connections

Do this sheet with your child.

Please read the following sentence twice to your child.

"The clown went downtown wearing a frown and a brown gown."

Questions:
"Who had a frown?"   *clown*
"Where did he go?"   *downtown*
"What was he wearing?"   *gown*

"Listen to me read these words: *brown, frown, gown, clown.*
What sound did you hear in each of those words?"

    "oun"

"That's right, 'oun' is at the end of each word.
Words that rhyme have the same sound in their endings."

"I'm going to read the *clown* sentence one more time. Each time you hear a word that ends in 'oun' I want you to make a big frown on your face." Reread the clown sentence.

"Please draw a picture of a clown with a frown."

clown   frown

"I'm going to read a sentence to you, and I want you to finish the sentence with a rhyming word."

"I smelled a red *rose,* when I held it to my _____."   *nose*
"Have you ever seen a *pig,* wearing a curly _____?"   *wig*
"I see a big *frog,* sitting on a brown _____."   *log*

"Remember the 'oun' family? What words end in 'oun'?" *clown, frown, gown, town, brown*

Do a rhyming riddle:
"What is a rabbit that tells a funny joke?"
"It's a funny bunny."

Here are some reading selections that highlight word families—rhyming words.

Hop on Pop by Dr. Seuss, Beginner Books, Distributed by Random House, 1963. Mr. Brown is upside down and other funny short stories. (Don't read this entire book in one sitting. Reread a couple of pages at a time. Make sure your child is looking at the print while you read. Ask him to fill in rhyming words when he is familiar with the short selection.)

Where's My Teddy? by Jez Alborough, Candlewick Press, 1992. Eddie goes searching for his lost teddy in the dark woods, and he comes across a huge bear with the same problem.

Rhyme With Me

Do this sheet with your child.

 Please read the following sentence twice *to* your child.

"A lady named Dot got another pot because the pot she bought was way too hot."

"What sound did you hear at the end of those words?"

          "ot"

"What words from the 'ot' family did you hear in that sentence?"

   Dot, got, pot, hot

 "I'm going to read *Dot's pot* sentence one more time. Each time you hear a word that says 'ot,' I want you to jump up as if your chair is hot." Reread the sentence.

 "Please draw a picture of a hot pot."

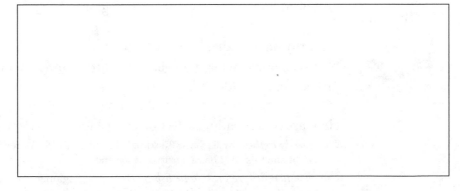

         hot   pot

"Now let's look at the 'ed' family. These words all end with 'ed.' Write *ed* in the spaces, and we'll read the words."

b<u>ed</u>

f_____

T_____

r_____

"Can you think of any other words that end with 'ed'?"

dead, head, Ned, said, wed

(Don't worry when word endings are spelled differently. Remember, as long as the word endings sound the same, they rhyme.)

"I'm going to read a sentence to you. I want you to say a word that rhymes to finish the sentence."

"Ben bumped his *head,* so he went to _____."	*bed*
"A lady named *Pat* wore a big black _____."	*hat*
"Tim took a long *trip* on the ocean in a _____."	*ship*
"A frog hopped and *hopped,* and got so tired it _____."	*stopped*
"I looked on the *rug,* and saw a big, green _____."	*bug*

Do a rhyming riddle:
"What happens when you get into a little car accident?"
"It's a fender bender."

Here are some reading selections that highlight rhyming words.

The Greedy Python by Richard Buckley, Scholastic, 1985. A greedy snake swallows lots of animals, and has a surprise at the end.

One fish, two fish, red fish, blue fish by Dr. Seuss, Beginner Books, 1960. One creature after another find themselves in silly situations. (Read a couple of pages at a time. See if your child can identify rhyming word families.)

Level 1 Reader

Rhyming Practice

Do this sheet with your child.

Please read the following sentence twice *to* your child:

"A bat wearing a hat had a chat with a cat who sat on a mat."

"What ending do you hear in the words of that sentence?"

"at"

"Now let's look at the 'at' family. These words all end with 'at.' Please write *at* in the spaces below and we'll read the words."

Level 1 Reader

c<u>at</u>

m_____

p_____

s_____

r_____

fl_____

"Can you think of any other words that end with the 'at' sound?"

bat, fat, hat, chat

"I'm going to read the *bat wearing a hat* sentence one more time. Each time you hear a word that ends in 'at,' I want you to pat your head." Reread the sentence.

👁 "Please draw a picture of a cat sitting on a mat."

cat   hat

👂 "Let's read these sentences, and I want you to say a word that rhymes."

I really like my *sled* because it's color is _____.   *red*

There is a little *mouse* who's running through my _____. *house*

If you look up in the *sky* you will see a bird flying _____. *by*

✍ "Let's read these sentences, and I want you to circle the word that rhymes."

Good-bye Animals

See you *later*, _____.   chipmunk   lion   alligator

See you *soon*, _____.   gorilla   raccoon   snake

See you in *awhile*, _____.   crocodile   whale   mouse

See you in a *few,* _____.   peacock   kangaroo   cheetah

See you in the *house,* _____.   sparrow   tiger   mouse

Do a rhyming riddle:
Example: "When camping, what can you sleep
inside that might be crooked?" "A bent tent."

Here are some reading selections that highlight rhyming words.

Cat Traps by Molly Coxe, Random House, 1996. A hungry cat tries to catch different animals without success.

Geese Find the Missing Piece by Marco and Giulio Maestro, HarperCollins Publishers,
1999. Animal riddle rhymes.

Improve Auditory Memory by Playing Memory Games

In addition to knowing how to rhyme, a child needs to have strong
auditory memory. This helps him remember word parts and put them
together. For example, e-l-e-ph-a-nt becomes *elephant*. It also helps a
child remember the sequence of a story that he is reading—otherwise
it won't make sense. A fun way to improve your child's auditory memory is to play games.

Visit My Aunt Memory Game

One of my students read the following sentences out loud. "You can
always tell when a cat is angry. A waving tail and flattened ears are
warning signs." (From *First Pets—Cats,* by Kate Petty, Gloucester Press,
1989.) When asked to review it, he said, "A cat has waving ears and a
flattened tail." *Hmmm.* He needed practice in remembering several
words in sequence. We played Visit My Aunt Memory Game for a few
sessions. It gave his memory and comprehension skills a nice boost.

*In order to read well, every child needs to have
a strong auditory memory.*

This game will help your child remember several words in the correct sequence.

How to Play

- Say to your child, "I went to visit my aunt in Kalamazoo. In my suitcase I brought my toothbrush."

- Then he says, "I went to visit my aunt in Kalamazoo. In my suitcase I brought my toothbrush and my skateboard."

- Now it's your turn, "I went to visit my aunt in Kalamazoo. In my suitcase I brought my toothbrush, my skateboard, and my hamster."

- Continue to add items until someone forgets an item, or says something out of order.

Add funny items like eggbeater, tire pump, or dental drill to make the game more fun.

This game can be played anytime, anywhere. Maybe your aunt wants to play!

Silly Command Memory Game

This game will help your child hold several directions in his memory. Practicing this will help him remember the order of events in a story that he is reading.

How to Play

- Ask your child to stand in front of you. Then give him two commands to do. "Jump up and down on one foot, then touch your nose."

- It is his turn to give two commands. "Scratch your back and untie your shoelace."

- When he is successful doing two commands, give him three commands. "Turn around once, touch the front door, and turn off the light."

- Now he gives you three commands. "Close your book, get a cookie, and do two sit-ups."

Remember: the sillier the commands, the better the game!

Good readers "see" pictures in their heads while they read.

Retell the Story Game

I told Daniel an easy three-part story one afternoon. First I said, "Daniel, I am going to tell you a story. I want you to remember it and tell it back to me.

'One day there was a man named Arthur.

He got on a city bus.

The bus took him to the zoo.'

Now tell the story to me please."

Daniel was unable to remember the story. He slowly mentioned two parts, out of order. What was going on here? This was a smart kid. I decided to tell him another story adding a visualization piece.

"Daniel, I am going to tell you a story. As I say each part, I want you to make a picture in your head. You're going to make a movie of what I am saying. Are you ready?"

I told Daniel a short story about a cat climbing a tree. After *each part* I reminded him to make a picture in his head. He retold the story perfectly.

Good readers "see" pictures in their heads while they read. It is likely that your child needs to learn how to create pictures in his imagination. This game will help your child learn to remember information by visualizing it.

How to Play

- Say to your child, "I am going to tell you a story. As I say each part, I want you to make a picture of it in your head, like a movie. Then you're going to tell it back to me."

- Begin by saying a two-part story, such as "I went to the store. I bought a cake."

- Be sure to prompt your child, "Describe your picture for me," after each part.

- When he can retell a two-part story, tell him a three-part story, and so on. Make the stories personal by including a favorite toy, pet, or friend.

You'll know his auditory memory is working great when he is able to visualize and remember a five-part story.

Learning how to rhyme and retelling stories will "prime" your child's ear/brain connection to get him ready for the next big step in reading—sounding out words. By the way, did you know that there's no word to rhyme with *orange?*

Information to Remember

○ Teach your child how to rhyme to increase his phonological awareness.

○ Play auditory memory games for a few minutes each day.

○ Teach your child how to remember a three-part story by creating pictures in his head.

○ Keep it fun, and your child will want to play again tomorrow.

CHAPTER 10

Better Letters

Beginning Reading

Hanna was a second grader. She knew letter sounds but she didn't know how to put them together to make words. A teacher told Hanna's mom that her daughter was borderline mentally retarded—based on an I.Q. test. I began to show Hanna three-letter words and taught her how to sound them out. In fifteen minutes she was beginning to read easy words: *hat, bat, cat, hot, cot.* Needless to say, the teacher was delighted to change her mind about Hanna's I.Q.!

Sounding out words is the beginning of a child's reading future. Some children spend more time in this phase than others do. Your child may breeze through this. Or, she may need lots of modeling and practice. Keep plugging away with the skills in this chapter until they are mastered.

Put Letters Together to Make Simple Words

When your child knows alphabet letter sounds, teach her to put three letters together to make a word. Many easy words are made of three letters with a vowel in the middle, such as:

cat   dog   mom   had   let   big   bus

See figure 10.1 for alphabet letter squares. Pull these two pages out of the book, and cut the letter squares apart. (*Consider getting the pages photocopied and laminated at an office supply store before cutting them apart.*) Letter squares allow a child to create words by herself.

This is an "aha," turning-the-light-on experience for your child. It begins as work and becomes a feeling of pride for your child as she becomes skilled at this exercise.

"Wynona, what does this letter say?" asks Mom as she points to letter *c*.

"k," says Wynona.

"Good," says Mom. "What does this say?" pointing to letter *a*.

"Aah as in apple," says Wynona.

"Now say the two sounds together, please," says Mom.

"Ka," says Wynona.

Mom says, "Here's an ending letter. What does it say?"

"t" says her daughter.

"Put the sounds together," says Mom. "What does it say?"

Wynona says, "Cat." | c || a || t |

How to Make Simple Words

Select the following letter squares (see figure 10.1): | c || t || p |
| n || b | and short | a |.

Show your child the first two letter squares of a word. | p || a |

Ask her to say the combined sound. | p || a |

Add an ending letter to form the word. Ask her to say the letter sound. | n |

Now your child should read the whole word. | p || a || n |

Here are more words to make from those letter squares:

can   cab   cat   cap   tap   tab   ban   bat   pat   nap

Train your child to focus on the first two letters in a word. Looking at the first two letters of an unknown word is a major reading strategy. If your child makes this a habit, her reading skills will improve.

Here are more combinations of letter squares to make into words. One short vowel is used in each combination. Children need lots of

Figure 10.1 Alphabet Letter Squares

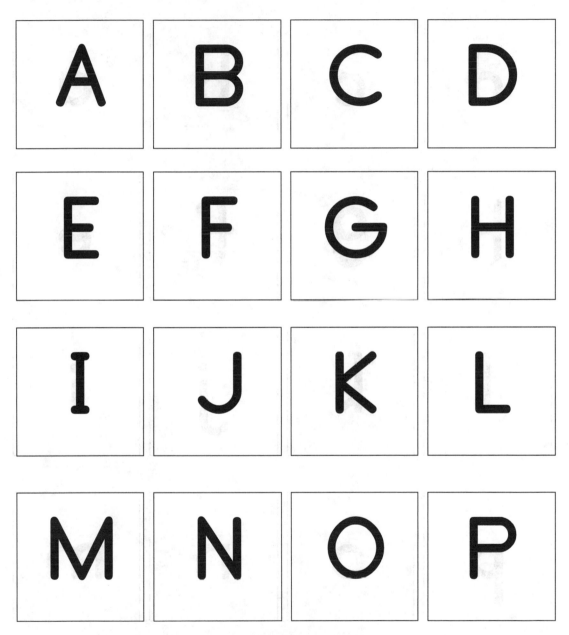

Figure 10.1 Continued

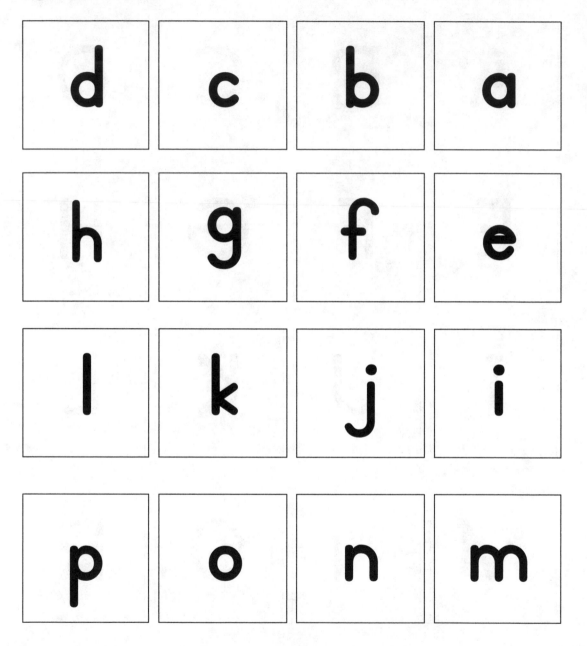

Q	R	S	T
U	V	W	X
Y	Z	a	a
e	i	o	u

t	s	r	q
x	w	v	u
a	a	z	y
u	o	i	e

practice with short vowels in order to learn them. Work with a set of squares until your child successfully reads all the words in each set.

Words that use **d, p, s, g, l,** and short **a:**

pad   pal   lag   lad   lap   sap   sag   sad   gal   gap   gas

Words that use **t, n, p, l, m,** and short **e:**

let   leg   pen   pet   men   met   ten   net

Words that use **t, s, h, p, d,** and short **i:**

hit   hip   hid   his   dip   did   dish   sit   sip   ship   tip   pit

Words that use **h, t, p, g, d,** and short **o:**

pot   pop   dot   dog   hop   hog   hot   got   top

Words that use **h, g, d, t, m,** and short **u:**

hug   hum   hut   dug   dud   tug   mud   mug   gum   gut

Level 1 Reader

Once your child has successfully made three-letter words with the short vowels, play some games.

Make the Word Game

The purpose of this game is to strengthen your child's ability to connect letters into words.

How to Play

- Say a three-letter word in its parts: "h," "a," "t"

- Ask your child to put the sounds together and say the word: "hat."

- Have her look for the letter squares that make the three sounds: *h, a, t*
- Ask her to say the sounds while pushing these letters together.
- Finally, have her read the word: "hat."

Some children will get part of the word correct, but not all of it. Instead of choosing letters *b, u, g,* for *bug,* Tina chooses *b, a, j.* Mom needs to model by saying:

"Tina, I said 'b,' 'u,' 'g.' Now I am going to put those sounds together," says Mom. "'b' 'u' 'g' says 'bug.' I'm going to look for the letters that say 'b' sound, and say 'u' and say 'g.' Here they are, letters *b, u, g.* Now, I'm going to put the letters together 'b' 'u' 'g.' Good! What does this say?"

"Bug," said Tina.

Mom says, "That's right!"

Attach Tails to Heads Game

This game gives your child extra practice in looking at the first two letters of a word—a good habit to cultivate.

How to Play

- Choose four (three-letter) words that your child can read.
- Set the letter squares up in front of your child so that she's looking at the beginning two letters of each word. For example:

b	a
h	u
d	i
l	a

- Ask her to read each of the beginnings out loud, to practice blending the first two letters.
- Give her an ending letter—out of order (p, d, g, t).

- Have her say the letter sound, and find a good beginning to attach the ending.
- Finally, ask her to read the words out loud: *bat, hug, did, lap.*

Ending letters might fit several beginnings. When she finds that the last letter won't fit, she'll have to rearrange some of the endings.

Helping your child read three-letter words leads to reading bigger words such as *Tyrannosaurus Rex*. That leads to reading sentences, which leads to reading books like *Anne of Green Gables*. And to think that it all started with "c" "a" "t"!

Information to Remember

To Make Simple Words:

○ Put two letters together. Ask your child to say their sound.

○ Add an ending letter to make a three-letter word.

○ Ask your child to read the word.

This is the beginning of sounding out words.

CHAPTER 11

It's Easy!

Reading Homemade and Predictable Books

> See Spot run.
> Run Spot run.
> See Spot run fast.
> See Mom fall asleep.
> —from Boring Books, by O. Yawn, 2005

Some beginning books are tiresome for both child and parent to read. They also insult the intelligence of older children. In addition, children who struggle in reading spend a longer time in the beginning phase of reading. They need stacks of easy reading materials.

I went to the library to search for beginning books. There weren't very many. Then I went to bookstores. Not many easy-to-read books there either. What's a body to do?

Make your own easy-to-read books! They're not hard to make, and you can save lots of money.

Create Your Own Pulitzer Winners

The beauty of homemade books is that your child is instantly successful in reading. Since the words come from his mouth, they are already familiar and are easily read (see figure 11.1). Best of all, they'll be a lot more interesting than seeing Spot run.

Figure 11.1 Roy's Homemade Book

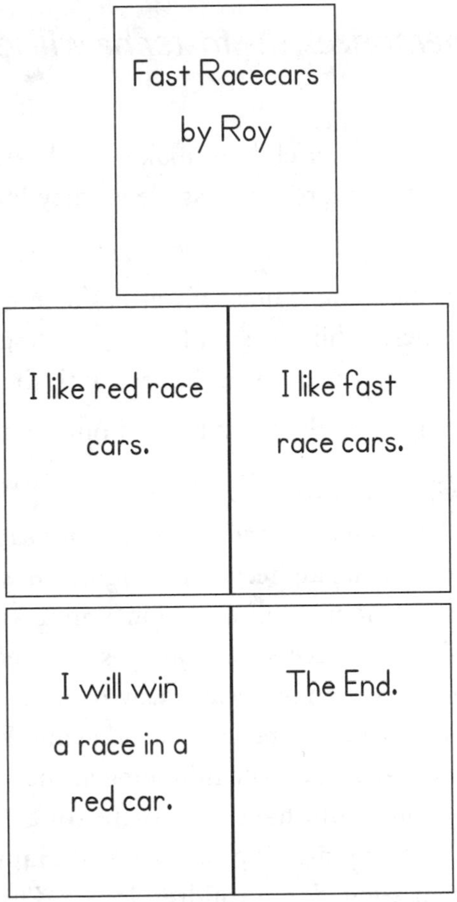

Fast Racecars
by Roy

I like red race
cars.

I like fast
race cars.

I will win
a race in a
red car.

The End.

How to Make an Easy-to-Read Book

- Put two pieces of paper together, fold in half, and staple the folded edge.
- Ask your child to choose a topic.
- Have him tell you a title for his book. Write the title on the front page.
- Your child will dictate three or four sentences to you. Write down one sentence per page. Write the words in clear large

Overuse of phonics is an inefficient way to read. The more written language a child memorizes, the faster he will learn to read well.

print. Help your child to make simple sentences and use as many of his words as possible so they look familiar.

- Let your child illustrate the pages.

- When the book is finished, sit beside him, and read it *to* him several times. While you read, run your finger under the words so he can connect the print he sees with the words you are saying.

- Now give him the book to read out loud.

He will read it pretty well.

"But he has memorized it!" you might say. When you read a newspaper, you are mostly recalling memorized words. On a rare occasion you dust off phonic skills to decipher an unknown word. For children, phonic skills are necessary to jump-start them into reading. But overuse of phonics is an inefficient way to read.

The more written language a child memorizes, the faster he will learn to read well—as long as he is looking at the words while reading them.

Does your child have a favorite song? Write down the words. Make a book by printing the lyrics of Happy Birthday. Every child knows that song. Some children love "What time is it when an elephant sits on your fence?" jokes. Help him make books about favorite animals, meals, toys, family members, or holidays.

Just in case you run out of ideas, here are a few more:

Topics for a Younger Child

I see a red	(or other colors)
I am waiting for	(or other feelings, such as I was sad when . . .)
What is cold?	(or what is hot, round, bumpy, flat . . .)
What starts with L?	(or other alphabet letter)
I like to eat	(or like to drink, play, watch . . .)

Topics for an Older Child

Places I Have Been
Our Pet Dog
My Best Friend
In my room there is a . . . .
On My Birthday

Create a book every two or three days. Keep them in a basket or box. Each day, ask your child to read two or three of his homemade books to you.

It's a Real Cut-Up!

"Tell me a sentence, Adam, about your visit with Grandma this weekend," I said.

He said, "I went to see Grandma, and we ate pizza and went to the movies."

"Good sentence!" I said. Then I wrote it down in clear print on a long strip of paper.

We read the sentence together several times. I took scissors and began to snip the sentence apart.

"Please read these pieces," I said to Adam.

"and we ate pizza" "and went to the movies." "I went to see Grandma," Adam said.

I snipped the phrases into words and asked Adam to read the separated words. Finally, we began to make silly sentences.

"Adam, read this," I said.

"The pizza ate Grandma and went to see the movies," he said. Then he made a quick rearrangement and read, "Grandma ate the movies and went to see pizza."

Making these sentences is a fun way to teach sight words, and sentence structure. Discussions about "Did that make sense?" and "How can we fix it?" can follow very silly sentences. It will help your child distinguish between sense and nonsense.

Read Predictable Books

Predictable books have repetitive segments that are easily learned, allowing children to "read" along with you. They help your child have instant success in reading fluently and memorizing sight words.

Here is an example:

Sam, why are there worms in your pocket?

Sorry, Mom, but I love worms and worms love me.

Sam, why is there gum in your hair?

Sorry, Mom, but I love gum and gum loves me.

—from *I Love Mud and Mud Loves Me,* by Vicki Stephens, Scholastic, 1994.

The best way to read a predictable book with your child is to sit beside him and:

- Read the book *to* him, running your finger under the words as you read.
- Read the book two more times and see if he can say a repetitive part *with* you.
- Read the same book once or twice a day until he can read it *by* himself, from memory, while looking at the words.
- Keep the predictable books together so he can read them at his leisure.

Here are predictable stories to jump-start your child into reading. Each story has a blank for your child to fill in (or he says the answer and you fill it in), making the story more personal for him.

Pull these stories out of this book and read them using *To, With, and By* (see chapter 4) until you are sick of spaghetti, birthday cake, and pizza. And until your child can say them while hanging upside down on the jungle gym or with his eyes closed at the breakfast table.

For each example, preteach words, using note cards, that he is likely to find unfamiliar (see page 139 for teaching sight words).

Predictable books have repetitive segments that are easily learned, allowing children to experience instant success.

I CAN   Preteach: dance   skateboard   spaghetti

I can run.

I can dance.

I can skate-
board.

I can slurp
spaghetti.

I can play
_____.

I can read
this story.

BABY EATS   Preteach: cake   peas   bananas

Baby eats cake.

Baby eats peas.

Baby eats
bananas.

Baby eats

_____.

Baby gets
messy.

Level 1 Reader

GOING UP   Preteach: rocket   helicopter   comes

A rocket goes
up.
A balloon goes
up.

A helicopter
    goes up.
A _____
    goes up.

A plane goes
    up, and
my Mom
    comes down.

ON MY BIRTHDAY   Preteach: candles   ice cream   presents

I had cake.

I had candles.

I had ice cream.

I had presents.

I had

_____.

I had fun!

THE CAR   Preteach: this   car   now   go

This is the car.

Dad got
    in the car.

Mom got
    in the car.
The dog got
    in the car.

The _____
    got in the car.
I got in my car.
    Now we can
    go!

MY LIZARD   Preteach: climbs   long   sleeps

My lizard runs.

My lizard has
    a long tail.

My lizard has a
    long tongue.
My lizard eats
    bugs.

My lizard
    _____.
My lizard
    sleeps.

THE BEST PIZZA   Preteach: sauce pepperoni   oven

We put sauce
on the pizza.
We put cheese
on the pizza.

We put
pepperoni
on the pizza.
We put _____
on the pizza.

We put the
pizza in
the oven.
We made the
best pizza.

NOISES   Preteach: cow   sheep   horse

What says
"Oink"?
A pig.
What says
"Moo"?
A cow.

What says
"Quack"?
A duck.
What says
"Baaa"?
A sheep.

What says
"Neigh"?
A horse.
What says
"_____"?
The farmer!

I SAW   Preteach: Tuesday   garbage   Thursday

Monday, I saw a dog.
Tuesday, I saw a garbage truck.

Wednesday, I saw a snake.
Thursday, I saw a bus.

Friday, I saw a
_____.
I like my new eyeglasses!

Level 1 Reader

Here is a small list of fun, predictable books to check out at your local library.

Polar Bear, Polar Bear, What Do You Hear? by Bill Martin Jr., Holt, 1991. Zoo animals make animal sounds and children imitate the sounds for the zookeeper.

Down on the Farm by Rita Lascaro, Green Light Readers, Harcourt Brace & Company, 1999. A girl can do activities just like her farm animals.

My Barn by Craig Brown, Greenwillow Books, 1991. Animals live in a barn making lots of sounds.

In the Spring by Craig Brown, Greenwillow Books, 1994. Animals are born in the Spring, on the farm.

My Puppy by Inez Greene, Let Me Read Series, Goodyear Books, 1994. A puppy is licking an African-American child.

Cat Traps by Molly Coxe, Step Into Reading Series, Random House, 1996. The hungry cat tries to catch different animals without success.

The Very Hungry Caterpillar by Eric Carle, Philomel Books, 1981. A hungry caterpillar eats his way through lots of food until he forms a cocoon around himself.

The Napping House by Audrey Wood, Scholastic, 1984. It's a wakeful flea that jumps on top of sleeping creatures, causing a commotion with one bite.

Information to Remember

○ Help your child create his own books to read.

○ Write down favorite songs and jokes for him to read.

○ Read predictable books with your child.

PART III

Rescuing a Level 2 Reader

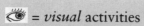 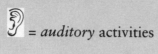 = *visual* activities

= *auditory* activities

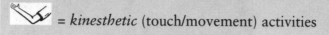 = *kinesthetic* (touch/movement) activities

Portrait of a Level 2 Reader

Emily was a talkative child with a great sense of humor. She finished second grade, having received special education services during the year. But she was almost two years behind in reading skills. Emily scored at fifth-grade level in science and history questions. Dad loved those subjects, and the two of them watched the history channel in the evenings.

During a special education meeting, teachers and Mom were making goals for Emily's next school year. Mom was disheartened to hear a teacher say, "Emily's problem is that she isn't trying very hard. If she paid better attention, I'm sure she could read better." Mom remembered her own troubles in school as a child. Was history going to be repeated here?

Testing showed that Emily knew most of the letter sounds except for *c, g,* and the short vowels. She slowly read twenty-five sight words and made several mistakes while reading a simple story. Her writing skills were minimal.

My goals for tutoring Emily would be to play auditory games and work on phonic skills. She needed to learn sight words, read lots of connected print, and write stories.

An optometrist checked Emily's vision and prescribed reading glasses. Every night Dad helped her write a short story, and they read short selections about animals and famous people using *To, With, and By.* Today she is a happy fifth-grader, reading at grade level, and scores at eighth-grade level in science and history. Emily was rescued from the effects and stigma of poor literacy.

CHAPTER 12

Half Hour to Power

Daily Reading Schedule

> "I sit beside her on the couch and she takes the first picture book from the
> bag.
> We read the story together, out loud, and when we finish one book we start
> a second.
> Grandma gives me a hug. 'Only seven years old and smart as paint already!'
> I'm pleased. 'They're all going to be so surprised on Saturday,' I say."
> —from the *Wednesday Surprise*, by Eve Bunting, Clarion Books, 1989

In this wonderful book, Anna does lots of reading practice with Grandma, getting ready for Dad's birthday party. At the party on the special day, Grandma stands up to read a book for her son. Dad is astonished because up to now his mom couldn't read. No one is *ever* too old to benefit from doing daily reading practice to become literate.

By now your child knows the letter sounds automatically. They are at the tip of her tongue. She's able to read three-letter words (see chapter 10 for review). Her reading skills will improve even if you do only fifteen minutes of *To, With, and By* per day.

However, there is a stronger, faster way to improve reading skills— by doing a daily half hour of an auditory game, writing, phonics, and reading connected print. See the Daily Half-Hour Schedule: Level 2 Reader on page 107.

Daily Half-Hour Schedule: Level 2 Reader

five minutes	Train the ears	(see chapter 13)
five minutes	Work on a phonic skill	(see chapter 14 and appendix A)
five minutes	Write a story	(see chapter 15)
five minutes	Learn sight words	(see chapter 16)
ten minutes	Practice Reading Time	(review chapter 4)

When the half-hour schedule is established, you both might be surprised at how time flies. Five minutes may seem short for some of these segments. Work quickly to keep your child on her toes, and change the order of activities to keep her interested.

Play a Game to Train the Ears [five minutes]

Successful readers have strong auditory skills—beginning with rhyming. If your child needs practice in rhyming, review worksheets and read rhyming books (suggested in chapter 9). She will learn other auditory skills by playing a game five minutes a day (see chapter 13). It's a fun way to help her hear the sounds of language better and create a strong foundation for reading success.

Work on a Phonic Skill [five minutes]

It's time to teach your child blends and twenty other phonic skills found in Appendix A. Each phonic set has a *Connecting Sound to Letter* sheet and three cartoon stories. Learning phonic skills allows your child to "break into the code" of words. She will absorb additional phonic skills by doing lots of reading practice.

Learning phonic skills allows your child to "break into the code" of words.

Level 2 Reader

We have to get out of driver's education class and into a car to apply driving skills, and the same is true for reading. Your child must open books and apply phonic skills to learn to read. Every time you do a *Connecting Sound* page together, have your child read the cartoon stories that accompany it.

Write a Short Story [five minutes]

Writing helps reading skills to improve. Help your child write a short story (three to four sentences) in her notebook every day (see chapter 15). Let her read her story over the phone to Grandma or give her a spoon, as a microphone, to read her masterpiece at the dinner table.

Learn Sight Words [five minutes]

Sight words are words your child miscalls, words you choose to preteach, or words from the One Hundred Most Frequent Word List (see chapter 16). Some children are able to memorize ten words per night, others work hard to learn three. No matter, go at a pace that allows *your* child to successfully learn sight words.

Practice Reading Time [ten minutes]

Begin the Practice Reading Time by letting your child show off. Ask her to read a short book or a story from her writing notebook. Because it's familiar, she should sound fluent while reading.

When your child has memorized a selection, challenge her by covering each picture, and ask her to read the words on the page. Then uncover the picture. This *forces* her to look at the print. Kids like this "game." Make sure this *warm-up* takes only a couple of minutes. Children want to stall here because it feels comfortable.

Today's new reading selection should be short—one or two *easy* pages or a paragraph—on your child's Instructional Reading Level. Help her read the selection using *To, With, and By*. (Review chapter 4 for choosing good reading selections and the *To, With, and By* technique.)

Keep her reading selections together in a cardboard box or basket. It will thrill your child to see the box fill up with books she can read by herself.

If you only have ten to fifteen minutes to work with your child today, which segment is most important? It's doing the Practice Reading Time—reading a new selection using *To, With, and By.*

Is there anyone else in your family who's willing to help when you are busy? Assign an older child to review sight words and read *to* her. Maybe your Mother can do a *Connecting Sound to Letter* page and cartoon story with her. Your child can read familiar stories from her notebook to the babysitter. Everyone can help in this important task.

Photocopy *Today's Worksheet: Level 2 Reader* (see page 110) to use in the next several weeks. Fill it out before beginning today's activities. The half hour will run more smoothly. Soon she'll be on a wonderful reading merry-go-round:

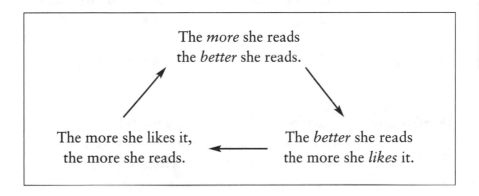

The *more* she reads
the *better* she reads.

The more she likes it,
the more she reads.

The *better* she reads
the more she *likes* it.

Level 2 Reader

Today's Worksheet

Level 2 Reader
Child's Name: **Date:**

[5 minutes]   **Play a Game to Train the Ears (see chapter 13)**
                Today's auditory game:
                Words to use in this game:

_____   _____   _____

_____   _____   _____

[5 minutes]   **Work on a Phonic Skill (see chapter 14)**
                Today's phonic skill (see chapter 14 or appendix A):
                The cartoon story (see appendix A):

[5 minutes]   **Write a Short Story (see chapter 15)**
                Today's story:

[5 minutes]   **Learn Sight Words (see chapter 16)**
                Review six to eight sight words on note cards:
                Sight words from today's selection:

_____   _____   _____

[10 minutes]   **Practice Reading Time (see chapter 4)**
                Read familiar story: (write down title)   Fluent? Yes ☐   No ☐

_____

                Read new selection: (write down title)   Fluent? Yes ☐   No ☐

_____

                Comments:

Level 2 Reader

Information to Remember

○ Make photocopies of *Today's Worksheet: Level 2 Reader* to help organize the half-hour reading time for each day.

○ If you only have a few minutes today, do a short selection with your child using *To, With, and By* (see chapter 4).

CHAPTER 13

In One Ear and in the Other

Connecting Ears to the Brain

When you pass a schoolyard and see kids playing jump rope, they are probably singing something like this:

Sally and Harry sitting in a tree,
k-i-s-s-i-n-g.
First comes love.
Then comes marriage.
Then comes junior in a baby carriage.

I bet you didn't realize they were doing games to train their own ears! Some children spend lots of time in the *auditory* (sound) world. They create silly jokes, make up songs, say sentences with words that all start with letter *b,* repeat funny poems, talk in pig Latin, and in general make you crazy while you are driving in the car. Their phonological awareness skills are strong.

Children who struggle in reading spend time in other worlds: They build things with their hands, draw fancy pictures, and want to play lots of video games. These children are also bright, but they are missing something.[1] It's up to the adults in their lives to introduce them to the auditory world, to build their phonological awareness.

A child needs to have strong auditory skills in order to learn phonics. Major phonological skills are:

- Rhyming (see chapter 9, *Rhyme Time*)
- Hearing differences between similar sounding letters such as *e* and *i* (as in *end* or *itch*)
- The ability to break words *apart* into separate sounds (*cup* becomes *c-u-p,* or *sheep* becomes *sh-ee-p*)
- The reverse ability to put parts of words *together* to make words (*d-r-i-nk* becomes *drink*).
- The ability to change words by replacing one or more letters to form other words (*can* becomes *cat; c*at becomes *s*at).

Games are the best way to increase your child's auditory skills. They can be played in the car while running errands, on the bus, or at the breakfast table. If you say, "Hey, let's play a game," that sounds more inviting than, "Hey, let's do some exercises for your ears," doesn't it?

Play a game for five minutes each day. Remember, games are supposed to be fun; stop before your child gets bored. You want him to say, "No Mom, let's keep playing." And you'll say, "We'll play again tomorrow."

These games are played with the ears, not the eyes. You'll be looking at words, but your child won't. He needs to rely on his ears to give the answers.

Same or Different Game

The purpose of the *Same or Different Game* is to teach your child to hear sound differences in word parts. I begin by having a child sit facing me. Once he knows how to play, I turn him so his back faces me.

A child needs to have strong auditory skills in order to learn phonics.

Level 2 Reader

When your child is successful in the Easy category, switch to the next one. Make sure he understands the meaning of "same" and "different." I received a lot of wrong answers until I taught children what those two words meant!

How to Play

- Say to your child, "Point your thumb up if these letters sound the same. Or, point your thumb down if these letters sound different."
- Be sure that you are saying the letter *sounds* of each pair, and not letter names.
- Refer to the Alphabet Chart (see figure 8.1 on page 62) for letter sounds.

Letter Sounds

EASY	MEDIUM	HARDER	BONUS
m-s	b-b	n-n	f-v
p-r	k-w	p-b	m-n
f-f	s-t	g-h	w-y (as in yo-yo)
j-l	r-l	z-z	g-g

The next category is hearing differences at the *beginning* of words. Watch out because your child might misunderstand and decide that words are the same because their endings rhyme. Explain to him and model the difference between *beginnings and endings* of words.

Say to your child, "Point your thumb up if the beginning sounds the same. Or, point it down if the beginnings are different."

Beginning Sounds

EASY	MEDIUM	HARDER	BONUS
cat-car	pup-pen	has-had	pug-bug
hand-hip	green-grew	bill-pill	shop-chop
red-let	hill-fill	clue-glue	when-where
pie-sip	stamp-stop	free-friend	class-glass

The next category is hearing differences in *endings* of words. Model a few pairs for him. Say to your child, "Point your thumb up if the endings sounds the same. Or, point it down if the endings are different."

Ending Sounds

EASY	MEDIUM	HARDER	BONUS
pin-pill	bag-bad	bib-bid	hand-bent
dog-dot	sat-hot	save-live	back-bank
ship-lip	rid-rip	gain-game	hatch-itch
fed-fell	men-ten	was(z)-pass	wish-lunch

The hardest category to differentiate is vowels—*a, e, i, o, u*—that are found in the *middle* of words. Consider these words: *bag, beg, big, bog, bug.* They have totally different meanings but similar sounds. A child might destroy comprehension by saying the wrong vowel sound: "The bag crawled up the wall."

Say to your child, "Point your thumb up if the middle sounds the same. Or, point it down if the middles sound different."

Middle Sounds

EASY	MEDIUM	HARDER	BONUS
hat-hot	man-men	bill-bell	bell-shawl
sap-soap	pot-put	bug-hut	blood-bled
hug-cup	dig-wig	strap-bat	coin-point
pail-pile	wet-best	cheese-street	had-head

Now create your own word pairs. Be sure to use one-syllable words. Write them on *Today's Worksheet: Level 2 Reader* (see page 110). Play this often and pretty soon he'll be all thumbs up in giving correct answers.

Take the Word Apart Game

I asked Tommy, "What sound do you hear at the beginning of *frog?*"
He said, "frog."
At least he's consistent with research about children who can't read, I thought. Some children hear a word as one unit. They don't hear the three parts of *fr-o-g* (frog).

Every child must learn that words are made of separate units. Teaching this skill may require modeling on your part. For example:

Mom says, "LeRoy, I am going to pull *starfish* apart into two pieces: star—fish." While she talks, she puts up a finger for each sound. "Now can you pull *skateboard* apart into two pieces?"

LeRoy says, "skate—board," and puts one finger up for *skate* and another for *board*. This game teaches your child how to break a word into separate sounds. When he realizes that words are made up of little sounds, he's one hop away from knowing that sounding out words is the act of putting those sounds back together.

How to Play

Begin this game with your child facing you. Once he knows how to play, turn him so his back faces you. This helps him rely on his ears. Each category gets progressively harder from breaking compound words apart to segmenting words into multiple sounds.

Easy: Compound word into two words. The Easy category is taking a compound word apart into its two words, such as "pea-nut" or "pop-corn."

Medium: A long word into two syllables. The Medium category is taking a word apart into syllables such as "yel-low" or "jump-ing."

Harder: A one-syllable word into two parts. Ask your child to take a one-syllable word apart by dividing the beginning of a word from its end such as "k-eep" or "fr-esh."

Bonus: One word into three or more parts. Ask your child to take a word apart by dividing it into three or more parts, such as "fr-ee-z-er" or "h-a-pp-y." (Please notice that doubled consonants such as *pp* or *ll* have one sound.)

Here are further suggestions for playing this game:

- I ask students to jump in the air for each part of a compound word or for each syllable in a long word. Older children like to put their fingers up for each word part.

- Be sure to exaggerate the word sounds—that is, say the word slowly, drawing it out. This highlights the different sounds. For example: the word *cool* is said, "kooooooooooollll." Your child should then say, "k-oo-l" and have three fingers up.

- Don't let him see your mouth (sit slightly behind him while playing this game). Help him take lots of words apart. Some words, such as *international* (i-n-t-er-n-a-sh-u-n-a-l), use ten fingers and a toe!

Take Words Apart

EASY	MEDIUM	HARDER	BONUS
eyeball: eye-ball	cookie: coo-kie	green: gr-een	bring: b-r-i-ng
earthquake: earth-quake	party: par-ty	mouse: mou-se	found: f-ou-n-d
airport: air-port	pizza: pi-zza	chin: ch-in	cream: k-r-ea-m
railroad: rail-road	supper: su-pper	tree tr-ee	strong: s-t-r-o-ng
sidewalk: side-walk	purple: pur-ple	brain: br-ain	drink: d-r-i-nk
backyard: back-yard	elbow: el-bow	car: c-ar	refrigerator: re-f-r-i-dg-er-a-t-or

Put the Word Together Game

While Randy was reading, he said: "My dog d-i-g-s, digs h-o-l-es, oles, leeses."

This is going from bad to worse, I thought. I realized that he'd forgotten the *h* of *holes* and missed the meaning of the sentence. Randy

Short-term memory throws information away if it's slow and fragmented.

needed to work on short-term memory, so we played the *Put the Word Together Game.*

Short-term memory throws information away if it's slow and fragmented. Your child might remember only two sounds at a time. You'll improve this by playing a game.

This game teaches your child to remember several *word parts* at a time—a wonderful skill for sounding out new words.

How to Play

Easy: Two words into a compound word. The easiest word units to say together are compound words. Say a compound word to your child in two parts, "flash-light," and your child says "flashlight." When he says compound words successfully, he's ready for the Medium category.

Medium: Two-syllables into one word. Words that contain two syllables are in the Medium category. Say "mon-key" and he says "monkey," or "pi-ckle" and he says "pickle."

Harder: Two parts into a one-syllable word. The harder category is when you say a one-syllable word in two parts: "c-ake" and he says "cake" or "gr-een" and he says "green."

Bonus: Three to four parts into one word. The final category is saying words in three or four parts. Tell your child, "I am going to say some sounds. I want you to put them together to make a word. Here's an example; I say 'm-on-st-er,' and you say 'monster.'"

Here are further suggestions for playing this game:

- Give him word-parts at a good speed—don't slow down.
- I clap *each word part* as I say them. Then the child says the word and claps *once,* signifying it is one word.

- I often look around the room to get ideas for words because they don't easily pop into my head. The list of words below can get you started.

Put Words Together

EASY	MEDIUM	HARDER	BONUS
mail-man	tur-key	sw-eep	b-o-x
hot-dog	blan-ket	b-ig	r-ou-nd
pan-cake	pen-cil	f-ast	f-i-sh
stop-light	spl-ash	st-ar	j-u-mp
night-time	fi-nish	tr-ain	d-u-st
tooth-brush	can-dle	cr-ash	f-u-nn-y

Level 2 Reader

Say other words in two or three parts. I played this game in the car while doing errands with my son. I gave him "W-en-dy's," or "Mc-D-on-ald-s," to put together. Let your child give *you* a word in parts to put together. (Just don't clap while you're driving!)

"Putting the word together" is *the major strategy* I use to help a child who can't decode a word while reading. For example, Brian is reading a short selection from *It's Best to Leave Snakes Alone* by Allan Fowler (Children's Press, 1992). He read,

"Some snakes are even helpful. They eat rats, mice, and other animals that d-de-demand farmers' crops."

I say, "That word is de-st-roy. Put it together."

"Destroy," he says.

"Do you know what *destroy* means?" I ask.

"It means they *wreck* stuff," he say.

"Okay," I say. "Now reread the sentence."

"They cat rats, mice, and other animals that destroy farmers' crops," Brian says.

Brian is more likely to read "destroy" correctly the next time, than had I just given him the word and moved on.

Make New Words Game

"Dewon," said Dad. "Listen to the word *smart*. Now, take away the *s*. What do you have?"

"Mart," said Dewon.

"Now take away the *t*, and put in a *k*. What do you have?" asked Dad.

"Mark," Dewon said.

"Good," Dad said. "Take away the *m* and add *sp*. What do you have?"

Dewon said, "Spark."

Dewon and Dad are having fun making new words by changing the first letters, last letters, and even the middle letters. The ability to manipulate and make new words is a complex phonological skill. Be sure to model this a number of times to ensure your child's success.

How to Play

Say a word such as *ball*. Tell your child "Take away the *b* and put in *t*. What do you get?" He should say *tall*. Don't leave a category until you're sure your child has mastered it.

Easy.   Replace the *first* letter of a word so that "*h*at" turns into "*m*at."

Medium.   Replace the *last* letter of a word so that "dog" becomes "do*t*."

Harder.   Change the *middle* vowels so that "p*o*p" becomes "p*u*p."

Bonus.   Change several letters at a time to make "*f*eet" into "*str*eet."

After using the words in table 13.1, choose other words from your child's reading selection to manipulate. He may want to take turns and give you directions to make new words.

The ability to manipulate and make new words is a complex phonological skill.

Table 13.1 Make New Words

EASY—BEGINNING LETTERS			HARDER—MIDDLE LETTERS		
dog	replace *d* with *f*	= fog	pat	replace *a* with *e*	= pet
cat	replace *c* with *b*	= bat	fin	replace *i* with *a*	= fan
hip	replace *h* with *l*	= lip	dug	replace *u* with *i*	= dig
bug	replace *b* with *t*	= tug	bent	replace *e* with *u*	= bunt

MEDIUM—ENDING LETTERS			BONUS—MULTIPLE LETTERS		
hop	replace *p* with *t*	= hot	crunch	replace *nch* with *sh*	= crush
bed	replace *d* with *g*	= beg	chop	replace *o* with *ir*	= chirp
pig	replace *g* with *n*	= pin	runs	replace *s* with *ing*	= running
sun	replace *n* with *b*	= sub	class	replace *cl* with *gl*	= glass

Getting Back into Connected Print

Here's frosting on the cake. Choose six to eight words from a reading selection, and say them in parts to your child. (Remember: he's not looking at the words yet.) Ask him to put the word together. *Now* help him find those words in the reading selection and read them to you. This is getting back into connected print.

Information to Remember

○ Play a game for five minutes each day to improve your child's ear/brain connection.

○ These games are for his ears; don't let him see the words.

○ Ask him to put words together. Then help him find and read those words in the selection.

CHAPTER 14

Reading Better

Using Phonic Skills

"My name is Ish.
I have this dish to help me wish.
If you wish to wish a wish,
You may wish for fish with my ish wish dish."

—from *One fish, two fish, red fish, blue fish*, by Dr. Seuss,
Random House, 1960

Doesn't this "sh" phonic selection tickle your ears? Dr. Seuss was a genius at making phonics interesting. We want to do the same thing for your child. Why bore her when there's a world of delicious language sounds out there? Connecting sounds to alphabet letters is the purpose of phonics.

If your child doesn't know what *e* or *i* says, she is going to have a problem combining *h-e-m* or *s-i-t* to make words. Her brain will process it h- -m, and s- -t. *Hem* could end up as *him, ham,* or *hum,* and *sit* could be *set* or *sat*. Worse still, are *hom, sot,* and *sut*—nonsense words that destroy comprehension. Without proper knowledge of letter sounds, especially the vowels, children do a lot of word guessing, hesitating, and butchering of easy stories.

Let's backtrack a little and analyze the act of reading. Today you picked up the morning newspaper and read the following item: "Montserrat's volcano exploded with a thundering cloud of ash that sent up incandescent rocks, and triggered avalanches of fiery boulders

> *Without proper knowledge of letter sounds, especially the vowels, children do a lot of word guessing, hesitating, and butchering of easy stories.*

down the mountain's flanks."[1] (Whoever said that newspapers were written at a fourth-grade level?) You may never have heard of a place called *Montserrat*. But you were able to read it by dusting off phonic skills learned so long ago.

Learning phonic skills in grade school began your journey into literacy. Knowing phonics helped you "break into the code" and read print. After awhile you picked up speed. With lots of reading practice you read using sight words, allowing for higher levels of comprehension. This is the most efficient way to read. But even today, on rare occasions you resort to using phonics.

Did you know that there are 166 phonic rules?[2] One obscure rule is: "oe at the end of a word says 'oo.'" That rule applies to one word—shoe. It's more efficient to learn *shoe* as a sight word. Learning all of those rules would create brain overload for your child. Her eyes would cross and smoke would pour out of her ears. Your ears might smoke too, if you try to teach her 166 phonic rules.

Children who struggle in reading may be able to learn phonic rules, but find it difficult to apply them during reading.[3] These numerous rules are more helpful for spelling. (Phonic purists, please forgive me.)

What phonic information is absolutely necessary to catapult your child into reading? Your child should know alphabet letter sounds (see chapter 8 for review), especially the short vowel sounds (a, e, i, o, u) and the "hard" sounds for letters *c* and *g*.

Your child needs to learn blends located in this chapter, and twenty phonic skills in appendix A. Don't try to teach them all at once—even if your child is in sixth grade. Each skill should be introduced and practiced in connected print. You'll have five minutes to work on phonics each day. That's enough time to play a blends game or do a phonics page and read a cartoon story.

> *Sounding out words is simply the process of linking letter sounds quickly enough to say a recognizable word.*

Teach Blends

Now that your child knows alphabet letter sounds, let's begin teaching her blends by using the *Blends Charts* and by playing games.

There's a new party game out called "Mad Gab" (Patch Products, 1995). One person reads a phrase out loud, such as "Itz Chris talk leer." She reads the phrase faster and faster while everyone else tries to decipher it before the timer rings. To play this game, people use *blending* skills—linking words together to say something that makes sense. (It's crystal clear!)

A blend is two (or three letters) that commonly appear together such as *bl, cr, st,* and *sc*. You can hear each letter sound in a blend. Lots of blends appear at the beginning, end, and middle of words, but not all need to be directly taught. Once your child understands the *concept* of blends, she can read additional blends. We'll focus on blends that occur at the beginning of words.

When your child blends the sounds of two letters such as *st, br,* and *fl*, she is practicing reading from left to right. This is an important step into *sounding out words*. Sounding out words is simply the process of linking letter sounds quickly enough to say a recognizable word. If blending letters occurs too slowly, a recognizable word might never appear. That's why your child must automatically recall alphabet letter sounds.

Blends Chart with Pictures

The following blends are commonly found at the beginning of words:

bl	cl	fl	gl	pl	sl	sc	sp
st	br	cr	dr	fr	gr	pr	tr

I teach blends by using a Blends Chart with Pictures (see figure 14.1).

 When using the chart, I may say, "Casey, look at these pictures, and listen to the sounds as I read them to you:

bl—blanket   *fr—frog*   *sc—scale*   *tr—truck*

Now, say the sounds with me as I point to the letters. Good job!"

Don't bother to use the word "blend" when you teach them. It's an unnecessary distraction. Just say, "Listen to these sounds as I say them to you." Be sure to point to the blend *letters* rather than to the pictures.

Introduce one or two blends at a time. Review them each day, by showing the chart and saying the sounds *to* your child and *with* your child. Ask your child to point to the letters (rather than the pictures) and say the blends *by* herself. Now play a game!

In the Ear Game

This game will help your child connect the blend sound to its letters. Even though she knows alphabet sounds, her ears need to recognize two letter sounds at a time. You might have to exaggerate both letter sounds such as saying "d-rrrrrrr," for the *dr* blend. The goal is for your child to recognize the blend when you say it at a normal speed. Make sure she looks at the chart, and not at your mouth. (Sit slightly behind her if necessary.)

How to Play

- Use the Blends Chart with Pictures and say a blend sound.
- Your child should repeat the blend sound—proving that she heard it correctly and point to the blend *letters,* not the picture.

Blend It Game

This game goes further in helping your child recognize and read blends.

How to Play

- Use the Blends Chart with Pictures (page 126) and begin by covering the pictures with pieces of paper.
- Say a blend sound.
- Have your child repeat the sound, then point to the blend letters.
- Show her that she is correct by removing the paper covering the picture.

Figure 14.1 Blends chart with pictures

Level 2 Reader

Concentration Game

Many blends look similar: *dr, br,* and *pr* or *gl* and *pl.* Your child needs to visually discriminate between blends quickly and accurately. Prepare materials for this game:

- Photocopy and if possible laminate the Blends Chart with Pictures and Blends Chart without Pictures (see figures 14.1 and 14.2).

- Cut them apart into squares. Every blend should have two squares: one with a picture and one without.

How to Play

- Choose four sets of blends (each set containing a blend with a picture, and one without the picture). Scramble the eight squares, and turn them face down.

- Take turns turning two cards over at a time, trying to make a match.

- Every time a card is turned face up, your child should say the blend sound, reinforcing her ability to read it.

- If two cards don't match, turn them face down again in the same place.

- If they do match, the player gets to keep the pair.

- The person with the most pairs wins.

As your child gets better at this game, add more pairs. Soon she will be able to play Concentration with thirty-two cards.

"Go Fish" Game

This game gives your child practice in recognizing and reading blends.

How to Play

- Use all the blend squares from both Charts to play this "card" game.

- Deal eight cards to each person. The rest go in a draw pile.

- Player #1 requests a blend card. "Do you have a *bl* card?" (Be sure to say the blend *sound*—don't name the blend letters.)

Level 2 Reader

- The other player hands over the requested card if she has it.
- The matched pair is placed in front of player #1.
- If player #2 doesn't have the blend card, she says "Go Fish!"
- Then player #1 takes the top card from the draw pile.
- The game ends when one person has no cards left in her hand.
- The player with the most pairs wins.

Figure 14.2 Blends chart without pictures

bl	**fr**	**sc**	**tr**
blanket	frog	scale	truck
cr	**st**	**cl**	**br**
crane	star	clock	broom
fl	**sl**	**gr**	**sp**
flag	slide	grapes	spider
dr	**pl**	**gl**	**pr**
drum	planet	glove	present

Put Blends into Connected Print

Open one of your child's favorite books. Ask her to find words that begin with a blend she has just learned. Help her read the words. Then read the page using *To, With, and By* (see chapter 4).

Phonic Skill Sheets

Phonics was not created as a medieval torture, similar to hanging by your thumbs. It has two important purposes: phonics jump-starts the process of deciphering print and frees a child from memorizing thousands of sight words. It's inefficient and impossible for a child to learn to read by memorizing every sight word in the dictionary. So teach her some phonic skills.

Appendix A, *Connecting Sounds to Letters,* contains twenty phonic sets. They are cleverly disguised as "Connecting Letter Sound" pages with three cartoon stories for your child to practice reading. Your child needs to master a phonic skill by applying it in other reading situations. However, this isn't work that your child can do on her own; she needs direct instruction from you to learn these skills.

The phonic sets are arranged from easy to intermediate levels. Even though you think your child might know these skills, don't skip anything. Use the sets as review.

If the skill sheets are hard for your child, don't sweat! Read and reread them to her. Over time, she will learn the phonic skills by practicing them in stories and other connected print.

It may take persistence and patience on your part to help your child learn a phonic skill. Remember that children need between four and fourteen exposures to learn and, more importantly, to *apply* a

Phonics has two important purposes: it jump-starts the process of deciphering print and frees a child from memorizing thousands of sight words.

skill. If she is mumbling sentences in her sleep she's ready to move on to the next phonic skill.

Pretty soon your child's phonic skills will be good enough that she will win at Mad Gab—It seezy asp I! (It's easy as pie!)

Information to Remember

○ Teach your child blends by using the Blends Charts.

○ Work on phonic skill sheets and stories with your child (see appendix A).

○ Practice each phonic skill until your child can apply that skill in other reading materials.

CHAPTER 15

Writing Right

Stories in a Notebook

Tom carried his notebook as he walked into my dining room. He was pleased because he had written two new stories and a knock-knock joke. He had also drawn pictures to go with the stories. There was a nice collection of stories and jokes in his notebook.

Reading experts are recommending that children do a short writing task every day.[1] They know that writing activities help your child's reading skills to improve. Writing is a language task that involves both visual and kinesthetic (touch/movement) styles of learning. Your child actively moves a pencil across paper and sees words that came from within his brain. It's easier for him to read words that he has just written than to read words composed by other people.

Some children resist writing because they are afraid of failing. It might be that your child doesn't know how to spell or he doesn't know *how* to write certain alphabet letters. All printed letters start at the top of the letter and *go down*. If he starts letters on the bottom line and goes up, help him write the letters correctly (refer to figure 8.3, Writing Chart of Lower Case Letters, on page 67). His writing will look better and be easier for him to read.

Writing is a task you must do *with* your child in order for him to develop writing skills. Keep it short, so that you stay within the five-minute time frame.

"What do you want to write about today, Tom?" I asked.

"Nothing," he said. (Even *my* students aren't always thrilled to write.)

"What's your favorite animal?" I asked.

Tom said, "I like lizards."

I said, "Cool. Did you know that lizards can grow new tails?"

"Yeah," he said.

"Let's write some facts that you know about lizards," I said as I opened his notebook to a fresh set of pages. See figure 15.1, Tom's Story.

To help your child write a short story, do the following:

- Get a spiral notebook and sit beside him.

- Have your child put his name on the front cover.

- Open the notebook to blank pages.

 • Have the child write on the left page (if he is sitting on your left), and you write on the right page.

- Ask your child to choose a topic. If he has trouble thinking of one, make a couple of suggestions (or see suggestions at the end of this chapter).

- Ask him to spell the title out loud *before* writing it down. If he spells it incorrectly, write the correct spelling on your page for him to copy. (Also show him that the title appears at the top, center of a page, and it needs to begin with a capital letter.)

Figure 15.1 Tom's Story

Tom's Page	Mom's Page
Lizard by Tom A lizard eats flies. A lizard lives in the desert. I like lizards.	Lizard flies desert

- Now have your child say one sentence at a time—what he intends to write. Ask him to spell each word out loud before writing the sentence. Fix misspellings by thinking out loud as *you* write them on your sheet. "When I say *lizard*, I hear an *l* sound at the beginning and a *d* sound at the end. Liiizzzard. Yep, I hear a *z* in the middle. The *i* comes after the *l* and *ar* comes after the *z. Lizard.* That looks right."

- The story should be three to four sentences long.

- When the story is finished, read it to him, running your finger under the words as you read.

- Now have him practice reading it.

Since many words in the English language break phonic rules, spelling is done with the eyes, not with the ears. This is the time for *modeling,* not making him "sound it out." If he sounds it out, it will be spelled "lizerd," and that doesn't look right. He'll learn from watching and listening to you model the correct spelling. Then have him copy the word into his story and read the story several times out loud. Lizard will be spelled correctly in the next story.

Don't worry if he wants to write bigger words like *Millennium Falcon* or *Throwbots.* He'll feel proud and empowered to be able to write them (with your help) and read them.

On the one hand, your child probably has enough brainpower to write four pages at a time in his notebook. However, his writing skills are at an emergent stage. Don't succumb to the temptation of making him write three paragraphs—you'll only get diminished results.

Try to remain true to his wording. Don't "substitute" easier words. He'll be able to read what he said because it came from his brain.

When he writes a short three-sentence story, with your modeling and support, he learns the following:

> *Since many words in the English language break phonic rules, spelling is done with the eyes, not with the ears.*

- how to write a title
- how to form alphabet letters
- words have spaces in between
- sentences begin with a capital letter
- sentences end with a period, question mark, or exclamation point
- sentences need to have a subject (noun) and a verb (action word)
- how to spell common words

Best of all, he becomes an author, expresses his own ideas, realizes that writing is fulfilling, watches his portfolio grow, *and* improves in reading skills as he rereads his stories until they sound fluent. This is one power-packed five minutes!

Research indicates that children who struggle in reading and writing have difficulty in recalling words.[2] This means that they need more *time* and *support* from us when we ask them to create sentences. That's how *their* brains function.

We want this activity to be fun for both of you, so let your child write jokes, silly stories, or rhymes. Ask him to draw pictures to illustrate the stories. Your child will be proud of his notebook. Encourage him to read his notebook to anyone who will listen. Keep a sense of humor and have patience as you teach how to spell and write during this activity.

One of my students had a great notebook in process. It was filled with stories and pictures. Unfortunately, a glass of water tipped over, drenching his masterpiece. Every page rippled and it became a sorry sight. So make sure your child's notebook is kept in a safe place, away from curious siblings and negative forces of nature.

Every time I tutor a student, I ask him to begin by reading two or three of his stories to me. Later, he will write something new in his notebook. The front of this notebook is a great place to put reward stickers.

Don't "substitute" easier words for your child's wording. He'll be able to read what he said because it came from his brain.

Writing Suggestions

Sometimes your child can't think of anything to write about. Here are some ideas:

I like (animal—such as eagle, iguana, elephant, gorilla, lion, snake, bugs, worms) because _____.

My best friend is (name). We like to _____.

This is how to play (game): _____.

If I were king for a day, I would _____.

One day I was sick and _____.

I like the (sports team) because _____.

My best birthday present was _____.

This is how to cook my favorite food: _____.

We went on a vacation to _____ .

Make a Short List

If you are going to Mars on a rocket, what do you need to bring?

What would you feed a monster for supper?

Invent a new sports car and describe its features.

How do you make a great pizza?

Describe your most perfect day.

Write two things about yourself that are true, and one thing that is false. Have an adult guess which one is false.

Answer a Question

What one thing in this world needs to be changed? How would you change it?

What do dogs dream about?

If the world ran out of gasoline, how would cars drive without gas?

What three questions would you ask your favorite sports player?

What are some differences between a dog and a cat?

What was the funniest thing you ever did?

What does your dad or mom do at work?

Figure 15.2 Short Story by Peter

Peter's Page	Tutor's Page
Fly Pudding by Peter You put dirt, rocks, sand, and lots of dead flies in it. You mix it. It tastes good.	dirt rocks dead flies tastes

Write a Joke

Kids especially like to write jokes that they've heard.

"Knock-knock" "Who's there?" "Boo!" "Boo who?" "Don't cry, it's only a joke."

"How do you get a down in football?" "You don't. You get down from a duck."

One of my students wrote a story (see figure 15.2) about making Fly Pudding. I don't think it tasted good, but it's creative, and *we're* proud of it!

Information to Remember

○ Give your child a spiral notebook for writing.

○ While he is writing today's story, help him by writing difficult words on the right hand page for him to copy. Model while you are spelling.

○ When he has written three to four sentences, ask him to read the piece to you.

○ Praise your child for his writing efforts

CHAPTER 16

Oh, See Can You Say?

Teach Sight Words

"There's a spider outside that would like to move in,
a pair of mosquitoes are riddling my chin,
the rat in the attic's determined to stay,
I'm facing a fairly *pestiferous* day."

> —from "There's a Worm in My Apple," in *Something BIG Has Been Here*
> by Jack Prelutsky, Greenwillow Books, 1990

Pestiferous . . . If you taught your child that sight word in the morning, it would be rolling off his tongue all day. You'd be sick of it by evening.

Sight words break easy-to-apply phonic rules and can't be sounded out. Think of *ocean, enough,* or *neighed*. If they were spelled phonetically, they would be *oshun, enuff* and *nayed*. More common sight words are *have* and *give*—that break the silent *e* rule.

Noah Webster, who created the first *American Dictionary of the English Language,* could have been more helpful by making all English words conform to easy phonic rules. But he didn't.

You want to teach sight words that get the biggest returns for your effort. They fall into these categories:

- Words your child can't sound out because they follow complex phonic rules or break rules

- Words that your child misreads

- Connecting words such as *into, with,* or *about*—which destroy comprehension when misread

Choosing Sight Words

Before your child reads a new selection, preteach three words. She will read the selection more fluently because they are already familiar. How do you decide which sight words to teach?

- Pick words to help comprehension or that appear often in print.
- Don't teach names of places or people such as *Yellowstone Park* or *Queen Elizabeth.* Instead, say those words in parts and have your child put them together.
- Choose words that can be "pictured." For example, words such as *tree* and *cow* are easier to learn than *can* or *the* because your child can "picture" what they represent in her mind.

Grandma chose three sight words to preteach to her granddaughter from the following selection:

"A polar bear can swim. A polar bear can dive under the ice.
A polar bear can sleep curled up. But a polar bear can't sleep upside down."
—from *A Polar Bear Can Swim* by Harriet Ziefert, Puffin Books, 1998

Grandma said, "The selection is about a polar bear so I will choose that." She wrote *polar bear* on a note card. "Lisa needs practice in silent *e* words, so we'll do *dive* and *ice*." She prepared two more cards.

"Look at these words, Lisa. I want you to listen while I read them," said Grandma. She held the cards up at Lisa's eye level and said each word clearly, flashing the note cards at a quick pace. Grandma reshuffled the cards and read each one again.

"This word is *dive*," said Grandma. "What does *dive* mean?"

Lisa said, "It's when you jump into the water with your hands first."

"That's right. Your hands and head go in first. You *dive* into the pool," said Grandma. "Show me what a *dive* might look like."

Lisa stood up and put her hands together over her head.

"Good," said Grandma. "Let's write the word in the air and spell its letters out loud—*d-i-v-e*. Oops. You were looking at me. Let's write it again, and this time look at the word. Okay?" said Grandma. "*D-i-v-e*. What's the word, Lisa?"

"Dive," Lisa responded. They quickly wrote the other words in the air while saying their letters.

"Now," said Grandma. "I'm going to show you the word *dive* again. Pretend your eyes are a camera. Take a picture when I snap my finger. Then close your eyes and put the picture into your head so you can see it. Are you ready?" asked Grandma. Lisa nodded. Grandma showed her the word and gave her two seconds to form a picture. She snapped her finger and lowered the card.

"Do you see the word?" Grandma asked.

"Yes," said Lisa with her eyes closed.

"What's the word?" asked Grandma.

"*Dive*," Lisa said.

Grandma said, "Good job."

How to Teach Sight Words

- Write each word in clear print on a three-by-five-inch note card.

- Hold the cards at your child's eye level, so she is looking straight across at them.

- Read each word to your child. Make sure she's looking at the note card and don't let her say anything at this time (kids tend to whisper the words).

- Read through the note cards twice, shuffling each time.

  These next steps stick words firmly in your child's memory.

- Read the words again, pointing out something significant about each word. Are there double *l*'s? Is a little word inside the bigger word—such as *ear* in *hear*? Or *far* in *farm*?

- Say, "Do you know what this word means? Can you put it in a sentence?" (If she doesn't know what it means, she won't remember it.)

- Can she act out the word?

- Ask her to write the word in the air *saying the letters out loud at the same time*. It's more fun if you do this *with* her. Or, invite her to write the letters on your palm as you both say the letters.

- Say, "Your eyes are a camera. Take a picture of the word and put it in your head."

- "Close your eyes. Do you see the word? What is it?"

- Now reflash the words again for two seconds each (one thousand one, one thousand two). It's important that your child recognizes sight words quickly—to promote fluency.[1] Children get used to this. They rise to the challenge and like to see how fast they can read the words.

One of my tutors talks fast. She moves quickly when she teaches sight words. She thinks of the child's brain as being a switchboard. The faster she talks, the more the child's switchboard lights up. In the final review, she flashes the note cards for two seconds. She forces her child to put words into visual memory. Her students have great success in learning sight words.

Put Sight Words into Connected Print

Mom taught Tiana three sight words. She flashed cards, had Tiana write words in the air, and put pictures of the words in her head. Tiana learned the words pretty well. Then Mom opened the book *My Puppy* by Inez Greene and said, "Tiana, look at this page. Find some of the words you just learned."

Tiana looked and said, "There's one."

"That's right," said Mom. "Read it to me."

"Licks," said Tiana.

It's important that your child recognizes sight words quickly—to promote fluency.

Mom said, "Now read the sentence."

"Okay," said Tiana. "My puppy licks my fingers."

"Good job," said Mom.

After your child has learned sight words, help her find them in the selection. Then have her read the sentences. Put the note cards into a baggie or little box to review the next day. When she has learned twenty sight words, remove them from the baggie. Give her a little reward and begin a new batch of sight words.

The One Hundred Most Frequent Words List

It is much easier for a child to learn words that create a "picture." But children must learn *connecting* words too. They don't carry much meaning but can destroy comprehension if miscalled. The list of words in table 16.1 is ranked in *order of frequency* from one to one hundred. *They make up one-half of all written print.*[2] If your child learns these one hundred words, in the same order, she will have a valuable foundation to draw upon when reading. Teach one or two at a time.

Here's how to teach them:

- Write the sight word on a note card. On the back, write a short phrase *from a reading selection* that includes the sight word. (It should be two to four words long; see figure 16.1.)

- Teach your child the sight word on the front and the phrase on the back (by writing letters in the air and making mental pictures).

- Open the reading selection and ask your child to read the phrase she just learned.

I'm sure you'll find other useful words to add to this one-hundred-word list. When your child learns these sight words, she will be a lot more fluent and less frustrated when she reads.

One Mom received a seventy-five-word list from her son's teacher. The teacher wanted him to learn them as quickly as possible because he was behind in reading skills. Mom was having very little success.

Table 16.1 List of the One Hundred Most Frequent Words Found in Print

Words 1–25	*Words 26–50*	*Words 51–75*	*Words 76–100*
the	or	will	number
of	one	up	no
and	had	other	way
a	by	about	could
to	word	out	people
in	but	many	my
is	not	then	than
you	what	them	first
that	all	these	water
it	were	so	been
he	we	some	call
was	when	her	who
for	your	would	oil
on	can	make	its
are	said	like	now
as	there	him	find
with	use	into	long
his	an	time	down
they	each	has	day
I	which	look	did
at	she	two	get
be	do	more	come
this	how	write	made
have	their	go	may
from	if	see	part

—From the *Reading Teacher's Book of Lists* by Edward Fry. Copyright © 1993. Reprinted with permission of Prentice Hall Direct.

Level 2 Reader

Figure 16.1 Teach Sight Words on Note Cards

give

give the dog

I asked her, "How are you teaching these words?"

She said, "Every night I sit down and go through all the words with him."

Uh-oh. This was brain overload! I said, "Teach your son one or two new words each night and review previous words. Don't do the whole list all at once."

Over time, her son was able to learn the list. After it had been broken down into small units, the impossible became possible.

Teaching Sight Words as Needed

Sometimes the word a child says looks similar to, but isn't the same, as a word in the book. For example, the word might be *are* and she said *ate* (see figure 16.2). (Many children confuse *was* and *saw*.) Misreading a word can destroy the meaning of the sentence. So you fix the word. But she misreads it again! Now it's time to stop and really teach her the word.

On one note card, write the correct word from the book—what she *should* have said. On another card write the word she *actually* said. Show her both words, side by side, and say, "How do these words look different? Which letters are different?" Have her explain the differences she sees between the words.

Teach her the words. "This is the word *are;* this is the word *ate.* *Are* has an *r* in the middle. Can you hear the *r* sound when I say *are?* *Ate* has a *t* in the middle. Can you hear the *t* sound when I say *ate?*"

Figure 16.2 Fix Confusing Sight Words

- Let your child highlight, with a pencil, differences she sees in the words on the cards.
- Now ask her to read the words out loud.
- Mix the cards up and have her read them again.
- Turn them face down.
- Ask her to turn one over and read it (this way she can't compare the letters on the cards).
- Sometimes, I go a step further and have her whisper the word, shout it, or say it in a growling voice or in a monster voice. After that, she won't be forgetting it anytime soon.
- Finally help her find the word *are* in the book and read the sentence. Add these cards to her baggie. It will take a few minutes to set those words straight for the rest of her life.

Miscalled Words

Sometimes a child misreads the same word again and again. Write it on a note card. When you have two or three note cards, stop the reading, and teach them to your child. Have her reread the selection correctly. Add these cards to her plastic bag too.

Sight words need to be learned to a "see it and say it" level.

Sight words need to be learned to a "see it and say it" level. It's wonderful when your child recognizes sight words faster than you are able to flash the note cards. Her reading will sound much better when she learns those pestiferous words!

Information to Remember

○ Teach sight words:

Choose three words from today's reading selection.

Write them on note cards and teach them to your child before she begins the selection.

Ask your child to tell you the meaning of each word.

Together, write each word in the air, saying the letters at the same time.

Help her put a picture of each word in her head.

Shuffle the note cards and flash them for quick recognition.

○ Teach other sight words as needed—especially ones your child miscalls while reading.

○ Review these sight words again tomorrow.

Level 2 Reader

PART IV

Rescuing a Level 3 Reader

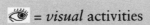 = *visual* activities

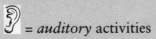 = *auditory* activities

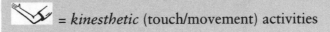 = *kinesthetic* (touch/movement) activities

Portrait of a Level 3 Reader

Dolores was a shy child at the end of third grade. Testing indicated that she read at a first-grade level. Her I.Q. performance was below average. Dolores lived with her Mom and an older sister near my house. Mom worked at a medical office to make ends meet.

Since her reading level somewhat corresponded to her I.Q. testing, Dolores didn't receive special education services. However, Mom thought that Dolores could do better. Her sister read well and Mom wanted help.

Dolores read half the list of first-grade sight words. I listened to her extreme effort in reading a story. Her phonic skills were in place, but not automatic. Dolores was unable to answer questions about the story she just read and her writing skills needed improvement.

The optometrist gave Dolores eyeglasses. I taught Mom and her junior high sibling how to do the *To, With, and By* technique. I also taught Mom some fluency and comprehension strategies.

In the afternoons, her sister did fifteen minutes of Reading Practice Time with Dolores. When Mom got home from work at night, she spent another fifteen minutes with her, working on fluency and comprehension strategies. With her family's help, Dolores was rescued from low expectations. She is able to read fluently with comprehension at grade level.

Now Mom saves a little money each month with plans that Dolores will go to college someday.

CHAPTER 17

Reading Well

The Final Frontier

"When I get a little money I buy books;
and if any is left I buy food and clothes."
—Erasmus, 1469–1536

Does your child feel that way about books? Are you frustrated because he cuts a wide path around them or treats them as if they're venomous snakes? One student used to cry crocodile tears whenever mom said, "Let's get to work." Now he is reading *The Hobbit*.

What made the difference for him? He gained the necessary tools to be a successful reader. It was a daily half hour of hard work—that progressively got easier. His mom gave consistent help, and they read lots of good selections from the library. Everything Mom did with him is in *Reading Rescue 1-2-3*, which is now resting in your hands. Now you have a Level 3 Reader in your house.

The daily half-hour schedule for a Level 3 Reader is as follows:

Daily Half-Hour Schedule: Level 3 Reader	
5 minutes	Learn three phonic clues (see chapter 18)
5 minutes	Write a short story (see chapter 15)
5 minutes	Learn sight words (see chapter 16)
5 minutes	Explain a fluency or a comprehension strategy (see chapter 19 or 20)
10 minutes	Practice Reading Time

This is a good time to give a retest (see chapter 6). What alphabet letter/sounds are not yet learned? Does he rhyme well? If not, review chapters 8 and 9 to get these important items hooked in his brain and ready for use.

Learn Three Phonic Clues [five minutes]

A Level 3 reader will learn phonic clues to use when deciphering unknown words (see chapter 18). Teach these clues one at a time and have your child practice them by reading lots of connected print.

If your child misreads words that contain *ea*, this is a good time to review that skill. Twenty sets of phonic *Connecting Sound* sheets and cartoon stories are available in appendix A.

Write a Short Story [five minutes]

Every child should do a writing piece every day—even if it's a joke or quick thank-you letter. If he is beginning *Reading Rescue on Level 3*, refer to chapter 15, *Writing Right*, to find out how to write short stories in a notebook.

Learn Sight Words [five minutes]

Choose three to five new words before beginning today's reading activities (otherwise you have lost precious minutes during the half hour). Select words that help comprehension. For example, if the story is about someone living on a ranch, make sure he knows the word *ranch*. (See chapter 16 to review teaching sight words.)

Explain a Fluency or Comprehension Strategy [five minutes]

Choose one fluency (see chapter 19) or comprehension strategy (see chapter 20) to implement. Explain the strategy to your child during this five minutes, so that you both are ready for Practice Reading Time.

Practice Reading Time [ten minutes]

Begin Practice Reading Time by asking your child to read a short selection from a book or story from his notebook. It's a good way

Level 3 Reader

to grease the wheels in his brain, getting ready for today's new reading selection.

Use one fluency strategy or a comprehension strategy to help him read the new selection so that it sounds good. Be sure to include at least one segment using *To, With, and By* (see chapter 4).

Does your child have homework? This is a good time to help him read a short selection to excellence from a homework assignment. You are killing several birds with one stone (not that you should kill any birds!). By choosing a reading selection from today's homework several things will happen:

- Your child will have better grasp of the information.
- He will learn important vocabulary and concepts.
- Your child will probably get a good grade from his teacher.
- More importantly, he'll feel pride in being able to answer questions in class.

A child is *learning to read* in the primary elementary years—kindergarten to third grade. From fourth grade on, he is *reading to learn*. Schoolbooks get progressively harder, educational expectations are higher, and teachers no longer give reading instruction in the classroom.

Your child needs help to get ready for this transition. I'm not suggesting that you do his homework for him. Instead, use this opportunity to model how he can approach homework assignments. He may surprise himself and like reading about wolf spiders or Jackie Robinson.

A child is learning to read *in the primary elementary years— kindergarten to third grade. From fourth grade on, he is* reading to learn.

Today's Worksheet

Level 3 Reader

Child's Name: Date:

[5 minutes]   **Work on a Phonic Strategy (see chapter 18)**
Today's phonic strategy:

[5 minutes]   **Write a Short Story in Notebook (see chapter 15)**
Today's story:

[5 minutes]   **Learn Sight Words (see chapter 16)**
Review six to eight sight words on note cards:
Sight words from today's selection to preteach:

_____   _____

_____   _____

_____   _____

[5 minutes]   **Explain a Fluency Strategy or a Comprehension Strategy (see chapters 19 or 20)**
Today's fluency strategy:
or
Today's comprehension strategy:

[10 minutes]   **Practice Reading Time**
Read familiar story: (write down title)   Fluent? Yes ☐   No ☐

_____

Read new selection: (write down titl)e   Fluent? Yes ☐   No ☐

_____

Was ____ the new selection too hard?   Yes ☐   No ☐

Comments:

Level 3 Reader

Level 3 Reader

Information to Remember

○ Give a retest (from chapter 6) to see what your child still needs to learn.

○ Make photocopies of *Today's Worksheet: Level 3 Reader* to help organize each day's half-hour reading time

○ If your child needs review in a phonic skill, redo the skill set in appendix A.

○ Teach the phonic clues one at a time and give him lots of practice in connected print.

○ Choose a fluency or comprehension strategy to focus on during Reading Practice Time.

CHAPTER 18

Use the Clues

Teach Three Phonic Clues

"We must go to your mailbox and look for clues," I said.

"How did you figure *that* out?" Annie asked.

"I, Nate the Great, have to think like a ... detective," I said.

—from *Nate the Great and the Crunchy Christmas,* by Marjorie Weinman Sharmat, Delacorte, 1996

There's nothing worse than to look at an unfamiliar word and have no idea how to decipher it. The opposite is also true: A child feels pride when she's able to figure out a troublesome word. How do you guide a child who is making futile attempts? Teach her how to *look for clues.*

You know the old adage: If you give someone a fish, she can eat supper. If you give her a fishing pole and teach her how to fish, she can eat supper the rest of her life.

You are "giving your child a fish" every time you read an unfamiliar word for her. She gets through the selection, but she hasn't learned any new words. It decreases frustration for both of you, but there's a better way.

If you teach your child how to look for *clues* in unknown words, you are "giving her a fishing pole and teaching her how to fish." She will be able to read independently some day. Here is what one dad said to introduce the three phonic clues to his daughter:

> *When your child uses clues, she moves beyond the slow "sounding out" phase of reading, into intentionally using strategies to decode words.*

"Jerisa, let's pretend you're a detective. What does a detective do?" Jerisa says, "She tries to find things and solve mysteries."

"That's right," says Dad. "You're the world's best word-solving detective. I'm going to teach you three special clues to figure words out. Let's learn one of them today."

Out of dozens of phonic rules, three clues emerge as being most useful. (If you spend time teaching your child *all* the phonic rules, you'll have to spend more time teaching all the exceptions to the rules—and English has lots of exceptions!)

When your child uses clues, she moves beyond the slow "sounding out" phase of reading, into intentionally using strategies to decode words.

Remember: she should be reading a selection on her Instructional Reading Level (see the 1:20 rule on page 27). Once a troublesome word is figured out and practiced, it becomes part of her literary vocabulary.

Teach your child phonic clues *one at a time*. Let her practice by reading lots of connected print before showing her the next clue. Now, let's look them.

Phonic Clue #1: Finger Blocking— Leaving the First Two Letters Exposed

Mom said, "Calida, when you come to a word you don't know, I want you to take this finger" (she points to Calida's right forefinger) "and cover the word except for the first two letters, like this . . ." Mom points to *fishing,* and helps Calida finger block it. Calida covered the word except for *fi*. "Now," said Mom, "get your mouth ready to say those letter sounds. What do they say?"

"*Fi*," says Calida.

Mom says, "Take your finger off and look at the rest of the word. It starts with *fi* because those are its first two letters. What does it say?"

Calida said, "fish-ing."

"Good. Please reread the sentence," said Mom.

 This clue is both kinesthetic and visual—your child uses her finger to cover most of the word. She says the beginning sound, uncovers the ending, and "pushes through" the word by sounding it out.

This decreases wild guessing because she has to look at the beginning of the word carefully. Children must be taught when and how to finger block. It takes lots of practice because they don't do it naturally. Expect to remind your child by "show and tell" on numerous occasions.

Phonic Clue #2:
Short Vowel–Long Vowel Sound

When you say the (short) vowel sound in a word and it doesn't make sense, try saying the vowel's name.

Jon read, "I will gaw (go) to the zoo."

Mom said, "What word didn't make sense?"

"Gaw," said Jon.

"That's right," said Mom. "Letter *o* does say *aw* (as in ostrich), but sometimes it says its own name. Read that word and make *o* say its name."

Jon said, "G-o, go."

"Good. Now reread the sentence," said Mom.

This clue can be shortened to, "Try the other vowel sound." It applies to words such as *go, find,* and *me.* Sometimes, the visa-versa is true. If the word doesn't make sense as a long vowel, try the short vowel sound such as *have, come,* and give.

Phonic Clue #3:
Look for a Smaller Word Inside

When you see a word you don't know, look for a smaller word inside. Seeing the smaller word might help you read the big word.

This clue can be shortened to, "Look for a smaller word inside." It applies to words with *re* beginnings or *ing* and *er* endings. Teach your child how to finger block parts of a word to look for smaller words such as re*act,* shorte*r,* know*ing,* or care*ful.*

Maybe the first couple of letters—the prefix—should be covered up. Or, she could finger block the ending letters—the suffix. Watch out, though: some prefixes cause the opposite definition of a word such as *dis*continue or *in*complete. As your child encounters different words, help her to analyze what beginnings and endings do to words. Sometimes the inside word sounds different, such as *or* inside of *word.* (If one clue doesn't work, she can move on to the next clue.)

Some children see a big word coming up and they freeze, causing a long hesitation. If your child knows this clue, she'll see a big word and right away begin to finger block, looking for a smaller word inside.

Find the Tiny Word Game

It's one thing to learn a strategy. It's another thing to apply the strategy. The purpose of this game is to give your child modeling and practice finding smaller words inside of bigger ones.

How to Play

- Open her favorite book.

- Both of you look for words inside of words.

- Finger block parts of a word and say the inside word.

- The person with the most words wins.

Did you see tiny words inside of words in this last paragraph? How about *tin*y, *favor*ite o*pen,* p*age,* p*lay,* and *beg*in? Little words are everyw*here!*

Applying the Three Phonic Clues

How would you help your child apply these clues? Let's look at some selections to find out:

Selection 1. This selection is for a beginning reader.

"Pat Pat They call him Pat.

Pat Sat Pat sat on hat.

Pat Cat Pat sat on cat.

Pat Bat Pat sat on bat.

No Pat No Don't sit on that!"

　　　　　　—from *Hop on Pop* by Dr. Seuss, Random House, 1963

Which sight words would you preteach? (Hint: They have unusual vowel sounds and one is a contraction.) I would teach *they, call,* and *don't* on note cards before reading the selection.

　　　　Phonic Clue #2, "Say the other vowel sound," is helpful for the word *No.* Most of the other words can be read by using **Phonic Clue #1,** "Finger block, and get your mouth ready to say the first two letter sounds of a word." You might have to remind your child that letters *th* say "th" for *that* and *they.*

Selection 2. The following selection is at a first-grade level.

"I was just born. I cannot see or hear, but I can smell.

I can smell my brother and sister close by.

We have downy fur to keep us warm.

We sleep most of the time."

　　　　—from *See How They Grow: Fox,* by Mary Ling, Dorling Kindersley, 1992

Which are sight words? It isn't clear-cut this time because there are more choices. Maybe your child can't read *brother* and *sister.* Or she needs to learn the meaning of *downy fur. Warm* and *born* are also valuable sight words to preteach.

　　　　Your child can use **Phonic Clue #1,** "Finger block, and get your mouth ready to say the first two letter sounds of a word," for many

Level 3 Reader

of the easier words. **Phonic Clue #2,** "Say the other vowel sound" is for the words *have* and *most.* **Phonic Clue #3,** "Look for a smaller word inside," will help with the word *cannot.*

This selection contains thirty-six words. If she miscalls more than two or three of them, it's on her Frustration Reading Level. She needs an easier selection to practice. We never know which words a child will find difficult on a particular day. That's why I am showing you how to apply phonic clues in several different reading selections.

Selection 3. This is at a second-grade reading level.

"At night, she walked for miles through the woods to get to the next station on the underground railroad. The journey north was long and dangerous. But there were many people to help her on her way."

—from *Young Harriet Tubman,* by Anne Benjamin, Troll Associates, 1992

Which words should be pretaught? Your child might freeze when reading the compound words *underground* and *railroad* because they are long words. She may not realize that they are easier to read when separated—*under, ground,* and *rail, road.* Other sight words are *journey, station, through, people,* and *dangerous.* Does she know their meanings? It'll be difficult to learn *journey* if she doesn't know what it means.

Phonic Clue #2, "Say the other vowel sound," is helpful for the word *she.* **Phonic Clue #3,** "Look for a smaller word inside," can be used for *walk*ed and *danger*ous.

Other words can be figured out by using **Phonic Clue #1,** "Finger block, and get your mouth ready to say the first two letter sounds of a word," and by paying attention to what makes sense in context.

Scaffolding

Teachers use a technique called *scaffolding.* (It's not what's used to paint their ceilings.) Scaffolding is introducing a new concept and providing lots of support to help the child learn it. As the student becomes

Scaffolding is introducing a new concept and providing lots of support to help the child learn it.

more competent, the teacher provides less support. Eventually, the student becomes independent and no longer needs her teacher's help.

We want to provide scaffolding for your child by teaching her three phonic clues, and helping her use them until she becomes an independent reader. Using a reading selection from *Alligators: Life in the Wild* by Monica Kulling (Golden Books Publishing, 2000), the following is what scaffolding looks like.

Mom pretaught the following sight words: *stomachs, alligator, stones,* and *digest.* Edie didn't know what *digest* meant, so Mom explained, "When an animal eats some food, the food goes in his stomach. The stomach breaks food apart into tiny pieces. This takes time and is called 'digesting.' Do you digest food, Edie?"

"Yes, but it sounds gross," she said.

"Find the word *digest* on this page and read it," said Mom.

Edie pointed and said, "Digest."

"Good," said Mom. "When you come to a word you don't know, finger block the end and get your mouth ready to say the first two letter sounds. Will you remember that?"

Edie nodded, "Yes."

Mom had already read the selection *To* and *With,* and it was Edie's turn to read *by* herself.

Edie began to read, "Some alligators have stones in their stomachs. The stones *grinned* up the alligator's food."

"What word didn't make sense?" Mom asked.

Edie said, "Grinned."

"Try saying the vowel's (i) name," said Mom.

"Grind," said Edie, and she reread the sentence. "The stones grind up the alligator's food so it is easier to digest. The stones have another use, too. They help keep the alligator . . . " and she stopped.

"Remember to finger block," said Mom.

Edie covered the word, and read as she uncovered it. "Un-der-water, underwater."

"Please reread the sentence," Mom said.

"They help keep the alligator underwater," said Edie.

"Okay," said Mom. "Read this selection to me one more time, and make it sound fabulous."

"Ma," said Edie. "I don't think digesting alligators can sound fabulous."

Mom said, "You know what I mean—*you* sound fabulous!"

Someday, Edie's mom will give little reminders such as, "Does that vowel make another sound?" or, "I see a tiny word in there."

With lots of practice, your child will automatically use phonic clues to figure out new words. She can use her own fishing pole to catch fish!

Information to Remember

○ Use three phonic clues to figure out unknown words.

1. Say the first two letters' sound.

2. Try the other vowel sound to see if it makes sense.

3. Look for a smaller word inside a big word.

○ Practice the clues by reading connected print

CHAPTER 19

Sounding Smooth

Fluency Strategies

One day Peter read a selection to me from *Dragon Gets By,* by Dav Pilkey (Orchard Books, 1991), and it sounded like this:

"WheneverDragonwokeupgroggyhedideverythingwrongFirsthereadanegg andfriedthemorningnewspaperthenhebutteredhisteaandsippedacupoftoast"

Peter didn't pause for commas or periods. He didn't stop to breathe. If I didn't stop him, he was going to turn blue!

Nonfluent readers spend all their time "calling words," using phonic skills as their only strategy for reading words. This work totally occupies their minds, leaving little energy left for comprehension. They can't answer questions such as "What just happened in the story?" or "What do you think will happen next?"

Fluency is reading smoothly at the speed of normal speech. A fluent reader *quickly recognizes words* in groups and comprehends what he has read. Knowing lots of sight words is essential for fluency. Using phonic skills to decode words should take a back seat, only to be pulled out on occasion.

A fluent reader quickly recognizes words *in groups and comprehends what he has read.*

Level 3 Reader

One of the biggest mistakes an adult makes is choosing selections on the child's Frustration Reading Level. (See page 27 for more information about reading levels.) Making a child read on his Frustration Level *destroys fluency*. The child gets used to sounding nonfluent and becomes convinced that he can't read fluently. Worse than that, the child's reading progress is impeded—he becomes frustrated and links reading with bad memories.[1] Why are we surprised when he doesn't want to do Practice Reading Time tomorrow?

Every selection that your child reads needs to be on his Instructional Reading Level—where he makes no more than one or two mistakes per twenty words. (The only exception to this rule is when the child has chosen a book and is highly motivated to read it. In that case I prefer to read the longer parts to him and let him read captions under the pictures.)

To, With, and By *Fluency Technique*

Remember *To, With, and By* is your single strongest strategy to improve your child's fluency. It's like the fairy godmother's magic wand. Using this simple 1-2-3 technique will make your child's words flow smoothly—like melted milk chocolate.

Using *To, With, and By* helps model how the selection should sound. As he listens to your reading, and practices reading with you, his ears get used to hearing fluent reading. When it is his turn, he will read fluently, with similar expression in his voice (see chapter 4 for review of the *To, With, and By* technique).

When I read with a child, I use different voices. A hungry lion voice sounds deep. A scared mouse sounds squeaky and high. It's more fun that way! Sometimes I stop a child's reading and ask, "Is that how you sound when you're mad?" or "How do you sound when you're excited?" After a while a reluctant reader will enjoy being dramatic.

Some selections lend themselves to drama, such as:

"Look out, Fish, there's a shark following you!"
"Only joking!" laughed the lobster.

"Look out, Eel, there's a great big shark following you!"

"Only joking!" laughed the lobster.

> —from *"Only Joking!" Laughed the Lobster,* by Colin West,
> Candlewick Press, 1995

Following are several other strategies to improve your child's fluency.

Have a "Fluency Talk"

Why not have a "fluency" talk with your child? We know that poor readers have auditory issues; their strengths often lie in other styles of learning, such as visual and kinesthetic. We also know that they learn best with direct instruction and lots of practice.

Fluency is an auditory concept. Your child can't see it, or touch it, and it has no smell. So teach fluency using a "show and tell" method.

Bob, a first grader, read a short selection nonfluently. Dad said to him, "I'm going to read this two different ways and I want you to tell me which one sounds better." Dad read the selection, imitating how Bob had read it, bumpy and breathy. Then Dad reread it sounding smooth and fluent. Of course, Bob liked the smooth reading better.

"Bob," said Dad. "Do you know what *smooth* means?"

"Is it like peanut butter that has no chunks?" asked Bob.

"Yeah! The second reading was smooth, wasn't it?" said Dad. "What other differences did you hear?"

"You breathed a lot in the first one," Bob said.

"That's right; and it sounded bumpy, didn't it?" asked Dad. "I'm going to read it again, and then it'll be your turn. Take one breath for each sentence and make it sound smooth because that's what good reading sounds like."

> *Fluency is an auditory concept. Your child can't see it, or touch it, and it has no smell. So teach fluency using a "show and tell" method.*

Your child is working so hard to read that he isn't aware of what it sounds like. When you hold up a "mirror" by imitating how *he* sounds, then show him *fluent reading,* he's more able to change his reading behavior.

A "fluency" talk is showing your child the target (fluent reading). You are giving feedback as to how to aim and how close to the bull's eye he is striking. Another form of feedback is using a tape recorder.

Tape Record Your Child's Reading

Children get excited when they hear themselves on tape—it's a great motivator!

- Record his first reading of a selection on a tape recorder or a video camera.

- Turn the tape recorder off. (Don't play it back to your child yet.)

- Read the same selection *with* your child and help him fix mistakes. Ask him to reread it several more times until it sounds good.

- Record your child's final reading of the selection.

It tickles children's funny bones to hear themselves read. In listening to both readings, they comment on mistakes in the first reading. Then they feel proud of their final reading. My students often want to take the tape home.

Time the Readings

Being timed while reading allows a child to compete with himself. This form of repeated reading helps your child to read more efficiently—maybe he'll stop breathing between each word or hesitate less often.

- Get a watch with a second hand.

- Time your child as he reads the selection the first time. Write down his time.

- Read the same selection *with* your child, helping him to fix mistakes.
- Ask him to reread the selection a couple of times *by* himself until it sounds good.
- Time him while he reads the selection for a final time.
- Compare the times.

Your child will enjoy beating his own time. He's learning to read more fluently in a fun way.

Record Favorite Books

Make your own "talking" books using a tape recorder. Make funny sounds signaling the end of a page. If the book is about a cow, then "moo." This tells the child to turn the page. Or if the book is about a pig, then "oink." Better yet, read it with your child sitting there and he can make the sound. This will be his favorite tape!

Before your child goes to bed, he'll listen to the tape and look at the book. He can listen in the car or at the babysitter's. This puts language into his ears and it models fluent reading. He will match the words he hears to the print he sees. My kids still haven't grown tired of them. In fact, they make their own tapes now.

Keep Your Place Marker

I was tutoring Lucas one afternoon and watching him read. His eyes were jumping all over the page. Kids like that often lose their place while reading. A place marker is the perfect tool for this problem.

There are different types of place markers. Some provide more support and some offer the minimum—so little, in fact, that most people aren't aware a child is using a place marker.

The place marker that offers the most support is a note card with a window. Cut out a window on a three-by-five-inch note card, allowing five words to be seen on the same line (see figure 19.1). This type of place marker reduces the distraction of surrounding print. It allows the child to read in phrases and not lose his place. If his eyes should glance at a picture, the place marker is a point of reference to come back to.

At first your child may resist using the window place marker, so model how to use it. Open his favorite book and begin reading out loud, using the place marker. Show your child how to move it along the line while reading. When I showed Lucas how to use the window place marker, he latched onto it and his reading improved immediately.

The next level of place markers is "line holders." Cut a manila folder strip nine inches long by three inches wide or use a business-length envelope. Put the place marker under the line that is being read, exposing the entire line. As each line is read, move the marker down.

Some people use rulers for this, but the multiple-inch lines and numbers are distracting (and we don't want to add distractions!). A "line holder" place marker decreases the amount of print a child sees at one time and keeps his focus on the line he's reading.

A place marker offering the least support is your child's finger. If he is right-handed, his finger should rest to the right of the line he's reading. When he has read that line, his finger moves down to the next line.

This is not the same as running a finger under the words while reading. I have met lots of children who open a book, hold the page

Figure 19.1 Window Place Marker

How much wood can a

open with their left elbow, and begin to stab at words with their finger while reading word by word. This finger-stabbing style promotes nonfluent reading. Holding a window or line place marker is a good way to occupy a child's hand and transition him out of stabbing words while reading.

When your child reads Instructional level selections fluently, the stage has been set for good comprehension. Fluency happens when your child has listened to lots of reading (modeling) and when he reads using *To, With, and By*. A tape recorder or a watch will also make positive differences in your child's fluency.

Fluent reading sounds good and sure beats r-ea-d-ing l-i-ke th-is. "A-nd I'm n-ot j-o-k-ing," s-aid the l-ob-st-er!

Information to Remember

○ Fluency is smooth reading.

○ Use the *To, With, and By* technique often (see chapter 4).

○ Tape record your child's reading.

○ Time his reading using a watch with a second hand.

○ Teach your child how to use place markers.

○ Fluency helps comprehension.

CHAPTER 20

Think About It

Comprehension Strategies

Comprehension is the goal of reading.[1] Up to now your child has been working on reading skills. It's like playing the piano—she's learned scales, knows rhythm better than a metronome, and reads musical notes. Now, she's ready to perform *Für Elise* by Beethoven. Better than that, she can interpret *Für Elise,* making her own impact on a song that's played in every recital hall in America.

Comprehension goes beyond reading print on the page. It is a creative thinking piece. It uses your child's prior knowledge—vocabulary and concepts already hooked in her brain, to help her *interact* with the information. A few children understand everything they read, even if read poorly. But a majority of struggling readers need direct instruction in comprehension skills.

In order to comprehend, your child must remember information *and* be able to manipulate it. She should be able to summarize, predict, create opinions, and defend them, based on information in the selection.

> *In order to comprehend, your child must remember information and be able to manipulate it. She should be able to summarize, predict, create opinions, and defend them, based on information in the selection.*

Your child is exposed to a bigger variety of words in the children's books that you read to her than from what she hears on prime-time television.

Increasing Vocabulary and Concepts

Remember that your child's *listening vocabulary* is the largest of her language skills. By reading interesting selections *to* her, you enlarge her reading and writing vocabularies. If she has *heard* a word before, especially in context (not on a spelling list!), it's more likely she will be able to recognize it and have greater comprehension.

Read nonfiction selections about jungle animals, the ocean, and the Civil War. Read *Tom Sawyer* by Mark Twain, *Sarah, Plain and Tall* by Patricia MacLachlan, or *Shiloh* by Phyllis Reynolds Naylor. Your local librarian is willing to recommend exciting books to read to children of any age.

Did you know that your child is exposed to a bigger variety of words in the *children's books* that you read to her than from what she hears on prime-time television?[2] That means *any* reading you do will expand her vocabulary more than conversations she hears on television.

Read to her at the supper table, before she goes to bed, waiting at the doctor's office, or on the bus. Read to your toddler or your middle school student. This will positively affect everyone's comprehension skills.

Introduce the Reading Selection

Let's say your child is reading a selection about St. Bernard dogs that rescue people in the Swiss Alps (*Barry: the Bravest Saint Bernard,* by Lynn Hall, 1973). Monks at a monastery train these dogs. If your child doesn't know about monks, St. Bernards, or the Swiss Alps, she won't understand this selection.

Before she reads the selection, take a two-minute "walk-through" to introduce new vocabulary and concepts.

- Look at the title—such as *Barry: the Bravest Saint Bernard.* Can she make predictions based on the title? Can she, for example, answer: "What might the dog have done to show he's brave?"

- Look at pictures in the book. "Why do you think there's snow on the mountains?"

- Find information about characters: their names and location. "Barry is the dog, and Werner is his trainer. It looks like they live near a church."

- Preteach sight words. For example, *monastery, avalanche,* and *rescue* (see chapter 16 for teaching sight words).

- Finally, ask her to find the sight words in the selection and read the sentences to you.

Now your child is well prepared to read the selection with good comprehension. You also taught her the strategy of doing a "walk-through" before she begins other reading selections.

Preteach a Sight Word and Concept

Teach your child one concept/vocabulary word *in greater depth* before she reads the selection. For example, I am teaching the sight word/concept *avalanche* as it occurs in *Barry: the Bravest Saint Bernard* and making a word wheel (see figure 20.1, *Avalanche* Word Wheel).

"Allysa, this is the word *avalanche,*" I said while writing it in the middle of a page. "What happens in *winter?*"

Allysa said, "It snows."

"That's right," I said. "Let's say it's snowing hard in the *mountains.*" (I write *mountains* and other important words in a circle around *avalanche.*) "Some people need to travel through the mountains. What might happen to them?"

"They'll get lost," said Allysa.

. "Right. Sometimes the *snow* becomes *ice*. Then more snow falls. The snow on top slides down. That's called an avalanche. What happens if the *snow slides* on top of people?" I asked.

Allysa said, "They'll get *stuck* under the snow, can't breathe, and get frozen."

"Yes, people can *die* in an avalanche. But they might survive if someone can *rescue* them," I said. "This story is about a brave dog who rescues people caught in an avalanche. He *smells* them and *digs* them out. Take a minute and draw a picture of an avalanche under my word wheel."

Making a *word wheel* and drawing a picture helps add a visual dimension to what you are saying. Now she'll know and remember the sight word *avalanche*.

Don't forget, children need between four to fourteen exposures before they remember new information. Even though you have gone into great depth in teaching her the word *avalanche*, your child might need several reminders. Don't throw the word map away—tape it into her writing notebook for future reference.

Fixing a Reading Mistake

Comprehension is deterred when a child says a word that doesn't make sense. Either she has created a nonsense word or the word is a wild guess.

Figure 20.1 *Avalanche* Word Wheel

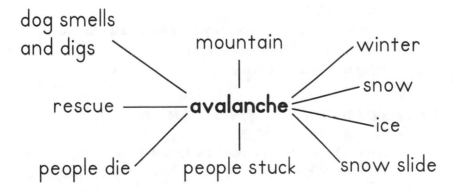

Carrie read the following sentence to me. "I went to the slarn to buy some bread." Then she kept on reading. I had never heard of a slarn. So I stopped her and asked: "Carrie, did that make sense?"

She said, "No."

Then I asked, "What didn't make sense?"

She told me, "Slarn."

"That's right," I said. "Let's go back and fix that word."

It's fascinating that some children make up words and continue reading as if nothing unusual has happened. But when I ask them, "Have you ever heard of a _____?," they laugh and say, "No." They don't stop to self-correct when they read. Miscalled words destroy comprehension and words that don't make sense *have* to be fixed.

"Did That Make Sense?"

When your child miscalls a word, let her finish the sentence. You want to see if she stops to correct herself. If she continues reading, stop her. Repeat the sentence she just said and say, "Did that make sense? Let's go back and fix that."

Remind your child of the clue: "Look at the first two letters and get your mouth ready to say their sound." (For review, see page 156.) She needs to say a word that begins with that sound *and* makes sense in the sentence.

If that doesn't work, give your child the word in two or three parts. For example, "That word is mon-a-ster-y." She puts the sounds together and says, "Oh, it's monastery," and rereads the sentence with the corrected word.

Some children will do anything to read a selection quickly, to get it over with, including making up words. If your child gets used to fixing words, she will make fewer wild guesses.

Create Pictures in Her Head

Susan, a third-grader, read a selection to me from *The Bravest Dog Ever: The True Story of Balto* by Natalie Standiford, 1989. She read it slowly and carefully. I asked her, "Why was the dog-sled team in such a hurry to get to Nome?" She didn't know—she had been "calling the words" without comprehension. I needed to help her "visualize" what she read.

When you and I read, we see pictures in our heads of the story as it's happening. Your child may not know how to do this, so you will teach her:

- Choose a reading selection and sit beside your child.

- Say, "Close your eyes. Inside your brain is a video camera. I'm going to read and I want you to make a picture of what I'm reading." Read two or three sentences to her.

- Stop and let her describe what she "sees" in her video. If she misses important information, reread sentences to her. (She should describe only what is written in the paragraph. Don't let her add unmentioned details because it may affect her comprehension.)

- Read the next sentences to your child. Have her add a second picture to the first picture in her head. Let her describe the second picture and review what she "sees" so far.

Do this five minutes per day—not any longer. You don't want to overload or frustrate her. If this is too hard, then model by reading a paragraph out loud. Close your eyes and describe to her the picture you "see" in your head.

Visualizing pictures and linking them together to recreate the story is a great way to improve comprehension. It takes effort on your part, but it is well worth it.

Summarize the Story

Before your child reads a short selection, tell her, "When you finish reading this, I'm going to ask you to tell me what's happening." This way she will pay attention while she is reading.

Sometimes a child will tell events from the end first, or will confuse details. Simply ask her to read it again. If it still doesn't make sense, make sure she understands the meanings of important words. Your child isn't trying to drive you crazy—she's actually missing important information.

I tutored an eight-year-old boy who was having difficulty remembering a selection about horses. I found out he didn't know what a horse's *mane* or *hooves* were. (I assumed he knew about horses because we live in Colorado.) I needed to teach these words to help his comprehension. Once I did that, he retold the story just fine.

If your child is unable to retell a story, play a game to improve her auditory memory. (For auditory memory games, see page 79.) After your child's auditory memory improves, she might even retell all of *Huckleberry Finn's* adventures.

Ask Questions

An excellent way to monitor your child's comprehension is to ask questions. Questions that you ask depend on the type of selection that she has read. Fiction selections are make-believe stories and nonfiction selections contain true information.

Questions for a Nonfiction Selection

Before your child reads a nonfiction selection, say to her: "When you're done I want you to tell me three things you learned." At first, she may not remember anything. Model how to do this. "Well, I learned that bears eat berries and fish because I saw a picture of the bear eating." Then open the book to the page so she can see it.

Children think that adults have a magical way of knowing things—as if you were born with this knowledge. When you model *how* to learn things, they quickly catch on. It takes only a couple of

An excellent way to monitor your child's comprehension is to ask questions.

minutes to model, and your child might even remember things that you didn't.

Questions for a Fiction Selection

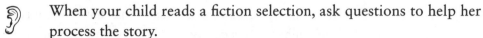

When your child reads a fiction selection, ask questions to help her process the story.

- "What do you think will happen next to _____ (the character)?"

- "Can you make a different ending?"

- "Tell me when something like this happened to you or someone you know."

- "What do you think is the lesson of this story?"

- "How would you change _____ (character) and how would that affect the story?"

Answering these kinds of questions will make your child feel important—you are asking her opinion. She gets to think more deeply than just retelling the story. If this is difficult for her, model how to answer these questions (she probably hasn't had much practice in thinking this way). And give her extra time to answer your questions.

These types of questions can lead a child into writing wonderful pieces. When she opens her notebook tomorrow, she may write a story that resembles today's reading selection with a new and fun twist.

Read a Story, Read a Recipe

On a regular day we read all sorts of material—street signs, maps, recipes, thank-you letters, bills, or reports. After getting up this morning, you might have opened the newspaper. You didn't expect to read baseball scores in today's weather section, or recipes in the obituary section. As you read, you adjust to different types of reading. This is a comprehension strategy.

Your child needs to adjust her expectations while reading, too. This comes with exposure to different types of print and lots of practice. Maybe she can read street signs or write up a food shopping list. She could help make brownies by reading the directions or read the comics out loud while you are washing the dishes. All of these activities reinforce the idea that reading needs to make sense and that reading is useful. After a while, she'll leave notes on the icebox saying, "Mom, don't forget to buy milk tomorrow. I love you."

Emily Dickinson penned the words "A book is like a frigate to take us lands away."[3] And William Miller affirmed that "Books are the road to the promised land."[4] As you help your Level 3 Reader grow in both fluency and comprehension, you are setting her well on the road to literacy—with the potential of going anywhere and becoming anything she wants to be. You have rescued her in reading!

Information to Remember

○ When your child makes up words, ask her: "Did that make sense?"

○ Before your child begins to read, make sure she knows the character(s) and where the story takes place.

○ Teach her to make "pictures" in her head while she reads.

○ Have her retell a story.

○ Ask questions when she finishes reading to help process information.

○ Comprehension is the ultimate goal of reading.

CHAPTER 21

Successful Strategies for School

To Make Everyone Happy

Precious children are sent off to school, with snacks in their backpacks as well as pencils and homework assignments. Most children race to the bus with a wave and a smile, looking forward to the day's activities. Other children trudge reluctantly to the bus because they find academics more difficult.

Implementing some strategies can transform your child from moaning about stomachaches in the morning to chowing down a bowl of cereal while announcing, "Mom, we're going to dissect a frog in school today. Isn't that cool?"

Do You Hear What I Hear? Following Auditory Directions in the Classroom

"Flamingo, Flamingo, what do you hear?
I hear a zebra braying in my ear."
—*Polar Bear, Polar Bear, What Do You Hear?* by Bill Martin Jr.,
Henry Holt & Company, Inc., 1991

All day long your child's teacher gives information, guidance, assignments, and compliments. Her voice competes with normal classroom sounds of shuffling feet, coughing, books being shut, and chalk scratching across a blackboard. Some schools have an "open classroom" setting where four classes share a common space, multiplying noises four-fold.

Some children have auditory processing issues—they can't retain auditory information. They also can't inhibit less important sounds.[1] One of my students, Jim, jumped every time he heard a noise from behind. He often looked around to see what was happening, thereby losing his place on the page as well as any comprehension he might have had. Because this also occurred while the teacher was talking, Jim had great difficulty in following her directions. He missed important information, such as homework assignments, and was performing way below his potential in school.

Does it seem that your child spaces out when you *ask* him to do something or says "What?" a lot? Does he insist that you said one thing when you said something else? If you are talking to him from across the room, is he unable to pay attention to you? Sometimes an attention deficit disorder (ADD) is an auditory processing issue in disguise or it occurs in tandem with auditory processing issues.[2] Although auditory processing issues can affect your child's classroom behavior, the good news is you can do something to improve them.

First, get your child's hearing tested either at school or by a pediatrician to rule out a physical hearing problem. Auditory disorders are sometimes caused by allergies that your child might have.[3] A good pediatrician or allergy specialist can address this. If the hearing test is normal, work with both your child *and* his teacher to improve auditory issues in the classroom environment.

Find the Sound Game

Your child's brain might not be strong at sorting and inhibiting normal classroom sounds. He might be unable to focus on the teacher's voice or what she's saying due to auditory distractions. This game will teach your child how to focus on the location of your voice amid other sounds; skills he can apply to the classroom setting.

How to Play

- Ask your child to sit on a chair and put a blindfold over his eyes.
- Stand in different parts of the room and call his name or say something witty.

- Your child should point to you.

- Let him peek under the blindfold to see if he's right.
- Add other sounds, such as turning on the television or radio, *one at a time*.
- Ask other children in the room to make noises. Your child should practice focusing on your voice and pointing to you. Have him repeat what you just said.

Ask your child's teacher if he could sit at the front or near where she is talking—away from other noisy sources. Set up a system where the teacher briefly checks with your child to make sure he understood her verbal instructions.

If an older student isn't grasping verbal homework assignments, ask the teacher to put them in writing or on the board for him to copy. I advise parents to have their child write down homework assignments, and then show it to the teacher after class and ask her to initial that it's correct. A good teacher won't mind doing this.

Your child can bring a set of earplugs to pop in his ears when he is concentrating on reading or a writing assignment. (Maybe it will become a fad with twenty-five children working quietly in their own worlds.)

Master That Spelling List

Terry comes home on Monday afternoon with a spelling list. He and his mom work together on it all week. But his mom notices that Terry is forgetting words he spelled correctly the day before. Terry's mom is upset because she knows their hard work should yield an *A* in spelling on Terry's report card instead of the *D* he gets each semester. Does this happen in your household?

> *Spelling words correctly is done through the eyes and not the ears.*

Your frustration is shared by hundreds of parents around the country! Spelling words correctly is done through the eyes and not the ears. If your child spells words based on what they sound like such as *wuz* (was) or *dun* (done), he will be in trouble—courtesy of the English language. He needs to learn what words "look like."

Teaching spelling words is similar to teaching sight words, with a few adjustments (see page 139 for teaching sight words).

- Teach your child four to five spelling words at a time. Don't try to teach all twenty words at one time or he'll experience brain overload.

- If he mixes up letters or omits letters, show him the note card and say, "Were you correct? Which letters weren't right?" He needs to compare what he said with what he sees.

- Ask your child to write the word (from the picture in his head) on a dry erase board. Then have him compare what he wrote to the note card. Let him decide if it's correct, and fix his own mistakes.

I Spy the Right Word Game

After your child knows most of the spelling words, add more visual reinforcement. Write the spelling list on a piece of paper and add two imposters for each spelling word.[4] For example, if the spelling word is *father*, you might write:

    fathur   father   fawther

Ask your child to circle the correct spelling. Show him the spelling list and let *him* correct any mistakes.

When considering your child's weekly spelling list, you may need to *negotiate* the following items with your child's classroom teacher:

- Spelling words should be chosen from his *current* reading selections—rather than a preordained grade-level list. These are more useful and are more likely to be learned well.
- Your child should be able to *read* the spelling words. Often children are given spelling words they can't read, much less spell.
- If your child is not a *self-primer,* he needs more time and support to learn spelling words. (For information about a child who isn't a self-primer, see page 12.) Therefore, it's appropriate to ask the teacher to choose half the regular number of weekly spelling words. Half a spelling list learned well is far better than an entire list learned poorly.

Above all, remember that spelling is a visual experience. Don't let your child "sound out" spelling words. Teach them to him in a visual way and he will ace the spelling test given each Friday.

To Read or Not to Read—Silently

Many years ago there used to be "blab" schools. Every child read his or her assignment out loud at the same time, and the teacher monitored the noise from her desk. Thankfully, that custom is outdated. Nowadays, children read silently in increasing amounts beginning in the first grade.

Silent reading is more efficient than reading out loud. Your child might have better comprehension when he reads silently. For these reasons, he should practice five to ten minutes each of reading out loud *and* silent reading when you work together on reading skills.

It's difficult to know what's going on when your child reads silently—so ask questions to monitor his comprehension (see chapter 20 for comprehension questions).

Your child might have better comprehension when he reads silently.

- Make sure the selection is on your child's Independent Reading Level—no more than one mistake per twenty words.

- Preteach important vocabulary words and concepts—giving him prior knowledge for good comprehension.

Silent reading is an important classroom skill that your child must develop. Join him in silent reading. He might become interested in your book someday.

Don't Take the Summer Off

Educators have a term for what happens to children who don't read in the summer. It's called the "Summer Drop-Off."[5] Children who like to read roar through a stack of books during the summer—thereby moving their reading skills forward.

Conversely, children who don't read have declining skills. Reading skills that aren't practiced are forgotten—it's not like remembering how to ride a bike. When these children return to the classroom in September, they have a greater distance to catch up.

On June 1 of each year, I set up a motivational system on a chart for my two children. For every ten books that they read, they get a reward: ice cream or a good used book from the local thrift store. This goes hand in hand with a family rule, "Everyone has to read at least half an hour every day."

Many libraries have summer reading programs with prizes and rewards. Call your local library to see what is being offered. Don't let your child experience a summer "drop-off." Instead, have a summer "jump-in"—jump into reading, that is. When your child goes back to school, he'll be bursting with valuable information gained from reading books and be ready to learn more.

Implementing these strategies will help improve your child's performance in the classroom. And then he'll say, "Mom, I think it's *so* cool when I get an *A* in school."

Information to Remember

○ Work with both your child and his teacher to improve auditory issues in the classroom.

○ Use a visual method to teach spelling to enable your child to learn spelling words more easily.

○ Help your child to practice a few minutes of silent reading every day.

○ Create a motivational system to help your child do lots of reading during the summer months so he'll be ready for school in September.

APPENDIX A

Connecting Sounds to Letters — Phonic Sheets and Cartoon Stories

Saturday morning Jeremy and his mom were sitting at the table working on the alphabet.

"Jeremy, what does the letter *a* say?" said Mom.

"A," he said.

"No honey," said Mom. "That's its name. What does short *a* say?"

"I don't know."

The only thing Jeremy knew about alphabet letters was their shapes: straight lines or curves. Mom needed to help him attach sounds to letters.

"Close your eyes, Jeremy, and make a picture of a huge letter *a*. Can you see it in your head? Good. Now put a picture of a big black ant beside the letter *a*. Do you see it? Okay, letter *a* says *aah* for ant. When I ask you, 'What does letter *a* say?' I want you to say 'a *aah* ant.' Tell me, what does letter *a* say?"

"a *aah* ant," said Jeremy.

"Good job," said Mom. "Let's look at your book, find *a*'s on a page, and read the words together."

Connecting an animal whose name begins with or contains an alphabet letter sound gives your child a "hook" to attach a sound to an alphabet letter. It's much easier for him to recall a *picture* from memory than a sound.

aah as in "ant"

Here are twenty phonic sets to work on with your child. Each set includes a "Connecting Sound to Letter Sheet" and three cartoon stories. The cartoon stories help your child apply the skill by reading connected print.

It's important that you do the Connecting Sheets and cartoons together—your child needs your help to make the connections, and he can't do it by himself. Teach the cartoon stories using *To, With, and By* (see chapter 4) until they sound fluent.

It may take several days for your child to fully connect the sound to the letter. Remember that you want to spend five minutes per day on this segment. Move quickly to keep your child interested.

These sets are intended to teach a skill your child does not yet know or strengthen an already acquired skill. A majority of struggling readers need to work on each of these phonic skills. Sometimes a child seems to know a letter sound but can't apply it while reading print. So, begin at the beginning and provide a solid phonic foundation for your child. Enjoy the process of making sound-letter connections!

A

Complete this sheet with your child.

Connecting Short A

Please read the following paragraph twice *to* your student.

"An ant had a bath. He made a big splash. Then he took a long nap. He rolled in the sand and had to take a bath again!"

Questions:
"What animal is in this story?" *ant*
"What did he take?" *bath*
"What did he roll in?" *sand*
"Listen to me read these words: *hat, man, dad.*"
"What same sound do you hear in these words?"
"That's right, letter *a* says 'aah' as in *f*a*n, b*a*t, *a*pple.*"
"Can you think of any other words that have an 'aah' as in *ant* sound?"

_____ _____ _____

"Please draw a picture of an ant taking a bath."

"Trace these letters five times."

"Now please read these words with me:"

and   as   pan

sat   dad   can

"When you see the letter *a*, what does it say?"   "aah as in ant."

"Let's read some sentences together:"

Sam has a van.

My dad ran after the cab.

Ants are on my back!

CAT   Preteach: has   on   happy

Cat has nap.
Cat has nap on mat.

Cat on lap.
Cat has nap on lap.

Cat is happy!

RAT   Preteach: after   catch   did

Rat ran.
Cat ran after rat.

Sam ran after cat.
Did cat catch rat?
Did Sam catch cat?

Sam has cat on his
lap.

ANTS   Preteach: want   find   like

Ants want a snack.
Ants find ham.

Ants like jam.
Ants go back home.

All the ants are glad.
Ham and jam are a
good snack!

Complete this sheet with your child.

Connecting Short E

Please read the following paragraph twice *to* your student.

"A elephant got out of her pen. Ted gave the elephant some lettuce. Then Ted put the elephant back in her pen."

Questions:

"What animal got out of her pen?" *elephant*

"What did Ted give the elephant?" *lettuce*

"Where did the elephant go at the end?" *pen*

"Listen to me read these words: *met, red, den.*"

"What same sound do you hear in these words?"

"That is right, letter *e* says 'eh' as in p<u>e</u>t, f<u>e</u>d, <u>e</u>gg."

"Can you think of any other words that have an 'eh' as in elephant sound?"

_____   _____

"Please draw a picture of an elephant eating lettuce."

"Trace these letters five times."

"Let's read some sentences together:"

I slept in a red bed.

"Now please read these words with me:"

get   red   men

leg   ten   yes

She has an egg in the nest.

"When you see the letter *e*, what does it say?"   "eh as in elephant."

The men got wet in the tent.

HEN   Preteach: hello   baby   chick

Red hen.
Ben fed hen.

Hen in nest.
Hen has egg.

Hen sits on egg.
Hello baby chick!

MEG'S LEG   Preteach: sled   bent   doctor

Meg is on a sled.
Meg fell off the
sled.

Her leg is bent.
Meg went to the
doctor.

He set her leg.
Meg must rest in
bed!

TED'S PET   Preteach: lays   cracks   open

Ted has a hen.
His hen is red.

His hen lays an egg.
The egg cracks
open.

The chick is wet.
Now Ted has
a new pet!

I

Connecting Short I

Please read the following paragraph twice *to* your student.

"An iguana likes to swim. He jumps into a river and swims fast. He is a swift river swimmer."

Questions:

"What animal is in this story?" *iguana*

"What does he like to do?" *swim*

"Where does he swim?" *river*

"Listen to me read these words: *sit, win, hip.*"

"What same sound do you hear in these words?"

"That is right, letter *i* says 'ih' as in *tin, six, his.*"

"Can you think of any other words that have an 'ih' as in iguana sound?"

_____   _____   _____

"Please draw a picture of an iguana."

"Trace these letters five times."

I   i

"Now please read these words with me:"

in   it   if

him   lid   big

"When you see the letter *i*, what does it say?"   "ih as in iguana."

"Let's read some sentences together:"

His big pig will win!

The king has milk on his chin.

Six sick chicks

(tongue twister—say it three times!)

TIM Preteach: under above sister

Tim hid.
He hid

under the sink.
Tim hid

above the swing.
Can Tim's sister
find him?

PIG Preteach: don't with kiss

This pig is big.
This pig will sit.

Don't sit on Tim!
Don't sit on Jim!

Here, sit with Kim.
Did that pig kiss
Kim?

FISH Preteach: race which more

This is a fish.
It is a big fish.

It has six fins.
When fish race,

which fish wins?
The fish with more
fins!

Complete this sheet with your child.

Connecting Short O

Please read the following paragraph twice *to* your student.

"An octopus has eight long arms. He hides under rocks along the bottom of the ocean. He is a long-armed, ocean bottom octopus!"

Questions:

"What animal is in this story?" *octopus*

"What does he hide under?" *rocks*

"What are his arms like?" *long*

"Listen to me read these words: *Bob, dog, mom.*"

"What same sound do you hear in these words?"

"That is right, letter o says 'aw' as in *top, fox, off.*"

"Can you think of any other words that have an 'aw' as in octopus sound?"

_____   _____   _____

"Please draw a picture of an octopus."

[ ]

"Now please read these words with me:"

on   not   frog

box   top   long

"When you see the letter *o*, what does it say?"   "aw as in octopus."

"Trace these letters five times."

"Let's read some sentences together:"

My dog is lost.

A frog is in my pocket.

I have a rock in my sock.

FROG   Preteach: frog   pond   away

| Frog can hop.
Hop frog hop. | Hop on log.
Hop off log. | Hop in pond.
Frog hops away. |

DOG IS HOT   Preteach: fan   Bob   is

| Dog is hot.
Mom is hot. | Bob is hot.
Fan is on. | Bob is not hot.
Mom is not hot.
Dog is not hot. |

TOM'S DOG   Preteach: spots   likes   new

| Tom got a box.
A dog is in the box. | The dog is from
mom.
The dog has spots. | Tom and mom walk
his dog.
Tom likes his new
dog. |

Complete this sheet with your child.

Connecting Short U

Please read the following paragraph twice *to* your student.

"I have an ugly umbrella. I have fun under an ugly umbrella in the rain and in the sun."

Questions:
"What does he have?" *umbrella*
"What does it look like?" *ugly*
"Where does he stand? *under*
"Listen to me read these words: *up, bug, mud.*"
"What same sound do you hear in these words?"
"That is right, letter *u* says 'uh' as in *p<u>u</u>p, h<u>u</u>t, <u>u</u>mbrella.*"
"Can you think of any other words that have an 'uh' as in *u*mbrella sound?"

_____   _____   _____

"Please draw a picture of an umbrella."

"Trace these letters five times."

"Let's read some sentences together:"

It is fun to hug a pup.
I just had lunch.

Gum is stuck to my thumb.

"Now please read these words with me:"

up   fun   cup
bug   cut   jump

CUB   Preteach: has   see   good-bye

Cub has fun
   in the sun,

in the mud.
See the bug.

Run cub run.
Goodbye cub.

CUB IN TUB   Preteach: mud   suds   has

Cub dug.
Cub dug in mud.

Cub in tub.
Cub in suds.

Cub has fun in
   the sun.

THE PUPPY   Preteach: puppy   tugs   pants

The puppy runs.
He runs to the bus.

He tugs at Gus.
Gus got mad.

Dust is on his pants.
But Gus hugs his
   puppy.

C

Complete this sheet with your child.

Connecting Letter C

Teach your child this connection by saying, "Letter *c* has two sounds. Most often letter *c* says 'k.' I want you to say the hard 'k' sound of letter *c* first. If the word doesn't make sense, then use the soft 's' sound."

Please read the following paragraph twice *to* your student.

"A camel likes to eat cookies. She cleans up the crumbs and closes her eyes for a little camel nap."

Questions:
"What kind of animal is in this story?" *camel*
"What does the camel like to eat?" *cookies*
"What did she do to the crumbs?" *clean*
"Listen to me read these words: *cub, care, coat.*"
"What sound do you hear at the beginning of these words?"
"That is right, letter *c* says 'k' as in <u>c</u>ap, <u>c</u>all, <u>c</u>orn."
"Can you think of any other words that have a 'k' as in camel sound?" (It is fine if your child says a word that ends in *ck,* because it has the same sound.)

_____   _____   _____

"Please draw a picture of a camel."

"Trace these letters five times."

"Let's read some sentences together:"

Can the cook cut the cake?

The cat had a cup of cream.

I like cotton candy.

"Please read these words with me:"

can	cut	cab
car	come	cost

CAT Preteach: come catch clever

Cat can sit.
Cat can nap.

Cat can come.
Can cat run?

Can cat catch?
Yes, cat is clever.

THE COOK Preteach: cookies crying cavities

This is the cook.
The cook likes
cake.

The cook likes
candy.
The cook likes
cookies.

The cook is crying
because he has
cavities!

CAT AND BIRD Preteach: carpet careful closet

Cat sees the bird.
The bird is on the
carpet.

Cat creeps to the
bird.
Be careful bird, or
cat will catch you!

The bird flies to
her cage.
Cat goes in the
closet.

G *Complete this sheet with your child.*

Connecting Letter G

Teach your child this connection by saying, "Letter *g* has two sounds. Most often letter *g* says 'g,' with the sound coming from the back of your throat. I want you to say the hard 'g' sound of letter *g* first. If the word doesn't make sense, then use the soft 'j' sound."

Please read the following paragraph twice *to* your student.

"The girl saw a grumpy goose. She gave him a gumdrop. The goose gobbled the gumdrop and gave her a grin!"

Questions:
"What animal did the girl see?" *goose*
"What did she give him?" *gumdrop*
"What did he give her?" *grin*
"Listen to me read these words: *gas, get, gum.*"
"What same sound do you hear in the beginning of these words?"
"That is right, letter *g* says 'g' as in *gift, got, game.*"
"Can you think of any other words that have a 'g' as in goose sound?"

_____   _____   _____

"Please draw a picture of a goose."

"Trace these letters five times."

"Let's read some sentences together:"

"Now please read these words to me:"

get   gas   gum
leg   got   hug

Gus got a gift.

I gave grandma a hug.

The goat ate green grass.

GO Preteach: said girl give

Go.
Go get.

Go get gum.
"Go get gum," said the girl.

I will get gum and give it to her.

GREEN EGG Preteach: what inside guppy

This is a green egg.
What is inside?

A guppy?
A gold bug?

I give up.
It is a frog!

GUS Preteach: eats growls other

Gus is a big dog.
Gus wags his tail.

Gus sits up and begs.
Gus eats bugs.

Gus growls at other dogs.
I will hug my big dog Gus.

Ch

Complete this sheet with your child.

Connecting Letters Ch

Please read the following paragraph twice *to* your student.

"My chicken is chirping. She lays an egg. A chick hatches from the egg. Now I have two chickens!"

Questions:
"What animal is in this story?" *chicken*
"What noise is she making?" *chirps*
"What does the baby chick do?" *hatches*
"Listen to me read these words: *chair, cheek, chop.*"
"What same sound do you hear in these words?"
"That's right, letters *ch* say 'ch' as in <u>ch</u>in, <u>ch</u>eep, ou<u>ch</u>."
"Can you think of any other words that have a 'ch' as in chick sound?"
(Make sure your child doesn't confuse "sh" words with "ch" words.)

_____   _____   _____

Read the following to your student. "Letters *ch* stay together as a pair and can't be split apart. They say one sound 'ch' as in chicken. Can you find any *ch* letters on this page?"

"Please draw a picture of a chick hatching out of an egg."

"Trace these letters five times."

"Let's read some sentences together:"

We ate chili for lunch.

I like to play chess.

How much wood did you chop?

"What does *ch* say? Now please read these words with me:"

chin   chap   chug

much   such   ouch

MY LUNCH   Preteach: chili   chocolate   another

I had some hot chili,
cheese and chips,

chocolate cookies,
and cherry pie.

That was such a
good lunch,
I can't chew
another bite!

CHICKEN POX   Preteach: chicken   itches   scratch

I have chicken pox.
It makes my skin
itch.

I scratch all day.
I scratch all night.

Mom put cream on
me.
Now all my itches
have gone away!

MY CHICK   Preteach: chased   munch   chirps

My chick is out of
her cage.
I chased her around
a chair.

I get some chips for
her to munch.

I catch her and she
chirps.
She is a silly chick!

Sh

Complete this sheet with your child.

Connecting Letters Sh

Please read the following paragraph twice *to* your student.

"I give my pet sheep a bath. I use shampoo. She shakes and I brush her. Then my sheep walks around the yard to show off."

Questions:
"What animal is in this story?" *sheep*
"What does he use to clean the sheep?" *shampoo*
"What does the sheep do after the bath?" *shows off*
"Listen to me read these words: *shop, shoe, shiver.*"
"What same sound do you hear at the beginning of these words?"
"That is right, letters *sh* say 'sh' as in <u>she</u>, <u>sh</u>out, <u>sh</u>ell."
"Can you think of any other words that have a 'sh' as in sheep sound?"

_____   _____   _____

Read the following to your student. "Letters *sh* stay together as a pair and can't be split apart. They say one sound 'sh' as in sheep. Can you find any *sh* letters on this page?"

"Please draw a picture of a sheep having a bath."

"Trace these letters five times."

"Let's read some sentences together:"

Is a shark a big fish?

The sheep sat in the shade.

She shut the door with her shoe.

"Now please read these words with me:"

ship   shed   shot

shy   dish   shak

MY SHADOW   Preteach: shadow   shake   shapes

I have a shadow
when the
sun shines.

My shadow is short.
My shadow is tall.
My shadow can
jump. My shadow
can shake.

What funny shapes
my shadow
can make!

A SHARK   Preteach: near   shiver   shy

I saw a shark.
It swam near my
ship.

The shark had sharp
teeth.
It made me shiver.

But this shark was
shy.
It swam on by.

THE SPLASH   Preteach: heard   should   light

I heard a splash in
the river.
Should I run with a
dash

to see what made
that splash?
I think it was a big
fish.

I will get a pole and
light,
to catch a fish for
supper tonight!

Th

Connecting Letters Th

Complete this sheet with your child.

Please read the following paragraph twice *to* your student.

"My mother puts her thumb up when I clean my room. This week she gave me three 'thumbs up.' I'll get more next week."

Questions:
"Who's happy when he cleans?" *mother*
"What does his mother put up?" *thumb*
"How many 'thumbs up' did he get this week?" *three*
"Listen to me read these words: *think, throw, thud.*"
"What same sound do you hear in these words?"
"That is right, letters *th* says 'th' as in <u>*th*umb, *th*ousand, bo*th*</u>."
"Can you think of any other words that have a 'th' as in *th*umb sound?"
Please read the following paragraph twice *to* your student.

_____   _____   _____

Read the following to your student. "Letters *th* stay together as a pair and can't be split apart. They say one sound 'th' as in mo*th*. Can you find any *th* letters on this page?"

"Please draw a picture of a thumb."

"Trace these letters five times."

"Let's read some sentences together."

I think I heard a thump.

He threw the ball over there.

There is a thorn in my thumb.

"Now please read these words with me:"

thin   with   third

the   teeth   this

THREE TEETH   Preteach: loose   pulled   brother

Three of my teeth were loose.

My mother pulled a tooth.
My father pulled a tooth and

my brother pushed a tooth.
Now I talk like thith.

MY BATH   Preteach: other   thin   bubbles

My brother had a bath.
My other brother had a bath.

Then I had a bath.
The water was cold.
The soap was thin.

There were no bubbles.
On Thursday, I want a bath first!

DOWN THE PATH   Preteach: python   slithered   I'd

I saw a big moth.
I saw a green sloth.
I heard a loud thud.

I saw a python in the mud.
It slithered past me.

All of these animals I'd rather see at my house on TV!

Wh

Complete this sheet with your child.

Connecting Letters Wh

(Whittle—to carve wood with a knife)
"An old man with whiskers liked to whittle whales. Sometimes whittling whales made him wheeze. He was a wheezing whale whittler."

Questions:
"What did the man have on his face?" *whiskers*
"What did he like to make?" *whales*
"How did he make the whales?" *whittle*
"Listen to me read these words: *when, whinny, wheat.*"
"What same sound do you hear in these words?"
"That is right, letters *wh* says 'wh' as in *where, whether, wheel.*"
"Can you think of any other words that have a 'wh' as in *wh*ale sound?"

_____   _____   _____

Read the following to your student. "Letters *wh* stay together as a pair and can't be split apart. They say one sound 'wh' as in *wh*ale. Can you find any *wh* letters on this page?"

"Please draw a picture of a whale."

"Trace these letters five times."

"Let's read some sentences together:

When can you fix my wheel?

Where is the big white whale?

Who likes to whistle?

"Now please read these words with me:"

when   whip   what

wheel   white   which

WHO?   Preteach: mouse   popped   hole

| "Who?" said the owl, "What?" said the mouse, | "Where?" said the snake, "Why?" said the fox | when the mole popped out of its hole. |

WHALE   Preteach: whaler   whacked   catching

| A whaler saw a whale | when he went out to sea. The whale whacked | his tail and said, "You won't be catching me!" |

WHY?   Preteach: whine   whisper   whimper

PLeeeeASE..

| I can't whack my sister. I can't whine to my mother. | I can't whisper to the baby. I can't wheeze on the cat. | I can't whimper at the doctor's. Why won't they let me do things like that? |

AI

Complete this sheet with your child.

Connecting Letters AI

Please read the following paragraph twice *to* your student.

"I saw a little snail on a rail. He left a wet trail. It began to rain. So I said goodbye to the little snail."

Questions:

"What animal did he see?" *snail*

"Where was the snail?" *rail*

"Why did he say goodbye?" *rain*

"Listen to me read these words: *raise, wait, paid.*"

"What same sound do you hear in these words?"

"That is right, letters *ai* say the name of letter *a* as in *main, bait, chain.*"

"Can you think of any other words that have an 'ai' as in snail sound?"

_____   _____   _____

Read the following to your student. "Letters *ai* stay together as a pair and can't be split apart. They say the name of letter *a* as in sn*ai*l. Can you find any *ai* letters on this page? What does *ai* say?"

"Please draw a picture of a snail."

"Trace these letters five times."

"Let's read some sentences together:"

A snail is in my pail.

He did not wait for the train.

I have red paint in my pail.

"Now please read these words with me:"

aid   aim   pain

maid   jail   brain

RAIN Preteach: brain straight down

Rain, rain, rain. This rain is a pain.	It's a pain on my brain.	I want all this rain to go straight down the drain!

SNAIL Preteach: began afraid wailing

A very sad snail began to wail.	"I am afraid I have no tail."	So the wailing snail fell into a pail.

PAINT Preteach: painted what fainted

I have a pail of paint. I painted a chair.	I painted my nails. I painted my hair.	Mom saw what I painted, and then she fainted.

EA

Connecting Letters EA

Complete this sheet with your child.

Please read the following paragraph twice *to* your student.

"Beavers like to eat leaves. They chew down lots of trees. Leave it to beavers to make a neat heap of trees."

Questions:
"What animal is this story about?" *beavers*
"What do they like to eat? *leaves*
"What do they make of trees?" *heap*
"Listen to me read these words: *eat, bead, lean.*"
"What same sound do you hear in these words?"
"That is right, letters *ea* say the name of letter *e* as in <u>*neat*</u>, <u>*heal*</u>, <u>*east*</u>."
"Can you think of any other words that have an 'ea' as in beaver sound?"

_____   _____   _____

Read the following to your student. "Letters *ea* stay together as a pair and can't be split apart. They say the name of letter *e* as in b*ea*ver. Can you find any *ea* letters on this page? What does *ea* say?"

"Please draw a picture of a beaver."

"Trace these letters five times."

"Let's read some sentences together:"

I eat jellybeans.

My jeans are clean.

It is easy to leap over a flea.

"Now please read these words with me:"

eat   sea   ear

read   meal   seat

MY EAR   Preteach: appears   peanut   year

Oh dear, it appears	I have a peanut stuck in my ear.	Will it be there until next year?

THE SEAL   Preteach: starfish   eaten   deal

In the sea there is a seal who is eating a nice meal	of starfish. The starfish thinks	it's a bad deal to be eaten by a seal!

I LIKE PEAS!   Preteach: speak   would   squeak

Please pass the peas. I eat lots of peas with my meat.	If peas could speak I am sure they would squeak,	"Don't eat us please. Just eat your meat!"

EE

Complete this sheet with your child.

Connecting Letters EE

Please read the following paragraph twice *to* your student.

"A bee flew to a tree. It buzzed to my cheek and sat on my knee. I think this bee likes me!"

Questions:

"What animal is this story about?" *bee*

"Where was the bee's first stop?" *tree*

"Where did it sit?" *knee*

"Listen to me read these words: *speed, deep, cheek*."

"What same sound do you hear in these words?"

"That is right, letters *ee* say the name of letter *e* as in <u>beef</u>, <u>cheese</u>, <u>keep</u>."

"Can you think of any other words that have an 'ee' as in bee sound?"

_____ _____ _____

Read the following to your student. "Letters *ee* stay together as a pair and can't be split apart. They say the name of letter *e* as in b*ee*. Can you find any *ee* letters on this page? What does *ee* say?"

"Please draw a picture of a bee."

"Trace these letters five times."

"Let's read some sentences together:"

Did you see the queen?

My jeep is on the street.

I see three monkeys
in a tree.

"Now please read these words with me:"

see   keep   meet

seem   need   week

THREE BEES   Preteach: heel   knee   climbed

My heel hurts.
My knee hurts.

My cheek hurts.
I was stung by three
bees.

I did not see those
bees
when I climbed the
tree!

GOODBYE BEE   Preteach: sneeze   after   flee

I see a bee. He is
near a tree.
Does the bee see me?

I need to sneeze.
Now the bee is
after me.

I must flee.
Goodbye bee. You
can't catch me!

SHEEP   Preteach: green   creek   under

Sheep eat.
Sheep eat green
grass.

Sheep drink.
Sheep drink at
creek.

Sheep sleep under
tree.
These sheep are easy
to keep.

Complete this sheet with your child.

Connecting Letters OO

Please read the following paragraph twice *to* your student.

"My tooth is loose," said the moose. "I'll pull it," said the goose.
So the goose pulled the loose tooth of the moose.

Questions:

"What was loose?" *tooth*

"Who's tooth was loose?" *moose*

"Who helped the moose?" *goose*

"Listen to me read these words: *mood, spoon, room*."

"What same sound do you hear in these words?"

"That is right, letters *oo* says 'oo' as in <u>roof</u>, <u>pool</u>, <u>boot</u>."

"Can you think of any other words that have an 'oo' as in m<u>oo</u>se sound?"

_____   _____   _____

Read the following to your student. "Letters *oo* stay together as a pair and can't be split apart. They say one sound 'oo' as in m<u>oo</u>se. Can you find any *oo* letters on this page? What does *oo* say?"

"Please draw a picture of a moose."   "Trace these letters five times."

"Let's read some sentences together:"

I wore my boots to school.

It will be afternoon soon.

The raccoon cleans his

"Now please read these words with me:"

food in the pool.

too	soon	good
moon	room	cool

ANIMAL MIX-UP   Preteach: rooster   loose   flew

"Honk," said the
cow.
"Woof," said the
goose.

"Moo," said the dog,
when the rooster
got loose.
"Woof," said the dog.

"Honk," said the
goose.
"Moo," said the cow,
"come back soon!"

IN THE WOODS   Preteach: raccoon   cleaning   animals

I looked in the
woods.
I saw a moose.

I saw a raccoon.
She was cleaning
her food.

Many animals are
in the woods.
I think I will come
back soon!

SLEEPING ANIMALS   Preteach: raccoon   rooster   cocoon

Is a moth up with
the moon?
Does a raccoon sleep
on the roof?

Is a rooster in a
cocoon?
No! A rooster sleeps
on the roof.

A raccoon is up with
the moon.
And a moth is in a
cocoon.

Complete this sheet with your child.

Connecting Letters OU

Please read the following paragraph twice *to* your student.

"There was a mouse in my house. I found him under the couch. I put him outside on the ground."

Questions:
"What animal was in the house?" *mouse*
"Where was he hiding?" *couch*
"Where was he put outside?" *ground*
"Listen to me read these words: *ouch, cloud, bounce.*"
"What same sound do you hear in these words?"
"That is right, letters *ou* say 'ou' as in <u>out</u>, <u>found</u>, <u>loud</u>."
"Can you think of any other words that have an 'ou' as in m<u>ou</u>se sound?"

_____   _____   _____

Read the following to your student. "Letters *ou* stay together as a pair and can't be split apart. They say one sound 'ou' as in m<u>ou</u>se. Can you find any *ou* letters on this page? What does *ou* say?"

"Please draw a picture of a mouse."

"Trace these letters five times."

"Let's read some sentences together:"

It is cloudy outside.

"Now please read these words with me:"

out   loud   our

sound   cloud   house

I found a hole in the ground.

The sound is loud!

THE MOUSE   Preteach: goes   come   couch

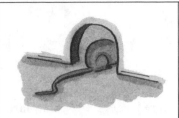

Out, out, the mouse goes out. In, in, the mouse comes in.	Shout, shout, Mom gives a shout	when she sees the mouse on her couch!

CAT AND MOUSE   Preteach: around   would   leave

In our house there is a mouse. In our house there is a cat.	Around the house runs the cat and mouse.	I wish the mouse would leave our house!

I CAN COUNT   Preteach: count   whisper   thousand

I can count in a whisper. I can count with a shout.	I can count to one thousand and ten or ten thousand and two.	I am a loud, proud counter. The best in my house!

Complete this sheet with your child.

Connecting Letters AR

Please read the following paragraph twice *to* your student.

"I saw a shark. It had a big scar. Its teeth were large. I hope that large scarred shark doesn't harm me!"

Questions:

"What did she see?" *shark*

"What did it have?" *scar*

"What size were its teeth?" *large*

"Listen to me read these words: *cart, hard, sharp.*"

"What same sound do you hear in these words?"

"That is right, letters *ar* says 'ar' as in *c<u>ar</u>, f<u>ar</u>, d<u>ar</u>k.*"

"Can you think of any other words that have an 'ar' as in sh<u>ar</u>k sound?"

_____ _____ _____

Read the following to your student. "Letters *ar* stay together as a pair and can't be split apart. They say one sound 'ar' as in sh<u>ar</u>k. Can you find any *ar* letters on this page? What does *ar* say?"

"Please draw a picture of a large shark." "Trace these letters five times."

"Let's read some sentences together:"

I park my car in the yard.

It is hard to march in the army.

A smart pig is in the barn.

"Now please read these words with me:"

car	part	hard
arm	yard	dark

STAR Preteach: shone wished large

A star was way up
  high.
It shone in the dark
  sky.

I wished upon that
  star.
I wished I had a
  large, red car.

But my dad said,
  "Of all the stars,
the star I chose was
  planet Mars!"

MY DOG Preteach: bark does neighbors

I hear a bark.
It is my dog, Clark.

He barks at stars.
  He barks at cars.

Clark must come in
  before someone
  yells at him!

MARK'S FARM Preteach: bull horns sharp

Mark has a farm.
He has a barn.

In the barn there is
  a bull.
On the bull are two
  sharp horns.

Mark has a sharp-
  horned bull
in his barn on his
  farm.

Connecting Letters ING

Please read the following paragraph twice *to* your student.

"A king gave a flamingo to the queen. She said, 'This flamingo is flapping its wings and is pink.' The king said, 'You will like this pink flamingo, I think.'"

Questions:

"Who gave the queen a present?" *king*

"What did he give her?" *flamingo*

"What was the flamingo flapping?" *wings*

"Listen to me read these words: *sing, cling, bring*."

"What same sound do you hear in these words?"

"That's right, letters *ing* say 'ing' as in *string, fling, and during*.

"Lots of action words have *ing* at the end like: *running, jumping, bouncing*."

"Can you think of any other words that have an 'ing' as in flam*ing*o sound?"

_____   _____   _____

"Can you find any *ing* letters on this page?

"Trace these letters five times."

ING ing

"Please draw a picture of a flamingo."

"Now please read these words with me:"

sing   bring   string

jumping   going   having

"Let's read some sentences together:"

I was sleeping in bed.

I was eating a snack.

I will get some string.

MY BROTHER   Preteach: hopping   bouncing   crawling

My brother is
   hopping.
My brother is sailing.

My brother is
   bouncing.
My brother is flying.

My brother is crawl-
   ing.
My brother is driv-
   ing me crazy!

EXCITING!   Preteach: shower   breakfast   exciting

Jump, jumping on
   my bed.
Sing, singing in the
   shower.

Run, running with
   my dog.
Bring, bringing in
   the paper.

Eat, eating my
   breakfast.
I'm having an
   exciting day!

MY HAMSTER   Preteach: waking   chewing   morning

In the evening
   my hamster
   is waking up.

He is running.
He is chewing.

In the morning
   he is sleeping.

B or D

Complete this sheet with your child.

"Is it a b or a d?"

Children confuse letters *b* and *d* because they still need practice with directionality—knowing left from right. Once your child knows his left hand from his right hand (see the Simple Simon game on page 225), he is ready to do this worksheet.

Please read the following information twice *to* your student.

"Did you know that you can make letters *b* and *d* with your hands? Your left hand makes a *b*. Your right hand makes a *d*. If you put an imaginary *e* in between, it makes the word *bed*." Show your child how to do this with his hands.

"When you can't figure out whether the letter is a *d* or a *b,* just make the word *bed* with your hands. Letter *b* is your left hand and letter *d* is your right hand."

"I am going to say letter *b* or *d,* and I want you to make your hand into the correct letter." d   b   b   d   b   b

"Let's look at some letter *d*'s and *b*'s. I will point to one, and I want you to make the same letter with your hand, and then tell me the name of the letter. Don't forget, your hands say the word *bed*."

d   b   d   d   b

"Please draw a picture of your bed."

"Trace these letters five times."

Practice Letters b and d—*Do this sheet with your child.*

Following left-right directions:

"Simon says, 'Pat your head with your right hand and rub a circle on your tummy with your left hand.'"

"Simon says, 'Hop on your right foot and pat your shoulder with your left hand.'"

"Simon says, 'Dribble a pretend basketball with your right hand and wave good bye with your left hand.'"

Use five colored markers to trace these letters.

"Make your hands into the word *bed* and read these words. (Remember that *b* is your left hand, and *d* is your right hand.)"

big   dog

bat   den

"Look! These words have a *b* or *d* at the end. You can read them! (Look at your hands if you aren't sure.)"

tub   hid

sad   web

"Some words have *d* or *b* at both ends!"

did   dad   bad   bed

"What's missing? Write the letter *b* in the spaces and read the sentence."

A ___ig ___ug ___it a ___oy.

"What's missing? Write the letter *d* in the spaces and read the sentence."

The ___og hi___ un___er the be___.

Which of your hands makes the letter *b*?
Which of your hands makes the letter *d*?

BAT   Preteach: sees   eats   goodbye

Big bat.   Big bat sees bug.   Goodbye bug.
Bug.   Big bat eats bug.   Goodbye bat!

DAN AND DOT   Preteach: den   find   found

Dan hid.   Dan hid in the bed.   Did dad find them?
Dot hid.   Dot hid in the den.   Dad found Dan
                                                       and Dot!

BASEBALL   Preteach: with   base   likes

Bob has a ball and   with his bat.   Bob ran to the base.
   a bat.   It was his best hit.   Bob likes baseball!
Bob hit the ball

SILENT E

Complete this sheet with your child.

Connecting Silent E

SHHH!

Please read the following paragraph twice *to* your student.

"When something is silent, it makes no sound. Silent *e* never makes a sound. But it is bossy. It makes the vowel in front of it say its own name!

Ask your child to read the following words out loud.

mad   cap   tap   can   plan

Now cut out the silent *e* square at the bottom of the page on the dotted lines. "What does silent *e* do to short *a* words?" Place the silent *e* square beside each word you just read, and read each word together again. (Mad becomes *made*, cap becomes *cape*, and so on.)

What's missing? Ask your child to fill in the blank spaces with the silent *e* square and read the sentence together.

The man mad____ a plan and built a plan____.

Ask your child to read the following words out loud.

her   Pet   hid   rid   dim

"What does silent *e* do to short *e* and *i* words?" Place the silent *e* square in the box beside each word and read each word together. (Her becomes *here*, hid becomes *hide*, and so on.)

✂

e

What's missing? Ask your child to fill in the blank spaces with silent *e* and read the sentence together.

Pet____ hid her pet mic____ and said, "Look what is sitting her____."

Ask your child to read the following words out loud.

hop   not   rob   con

"What does silent *e* do to short *o* words?" Place the silent *e* square in the box beside each word and read each word together. (Hop becomes *hope*, not becomes *note*, and so on.)

What's missing? Ask your child to fill in the blank spaces with silent *e* and read the sentence together.

Rob wok____ up and put on his rob____.

Ask your child to read the following words out loud.

tub   cut   hug   tun

"What does silent *e* do to short *u* words?" Place the silent *e* square in the box beside each word and read each word together. (Cut becomes *cute,* hug becomes *huge*—notice that the *g* changes to its soft "j" sound. Letter *c* also changes to its soft "s" sound.)

What's missing? Ask your child to fill in the blank spaces with silent *e* and read the sentence together.

The bear cub lik____d having ic____ cub____s in the bathtub.

e

Help the Snake with Silent E—*Do this sheet with your child.*

"Joe the snake wants to go home to his hole. You can help him get there!"

Directions: Put your silent e square in the square beside each word, and read the word out loud.

START

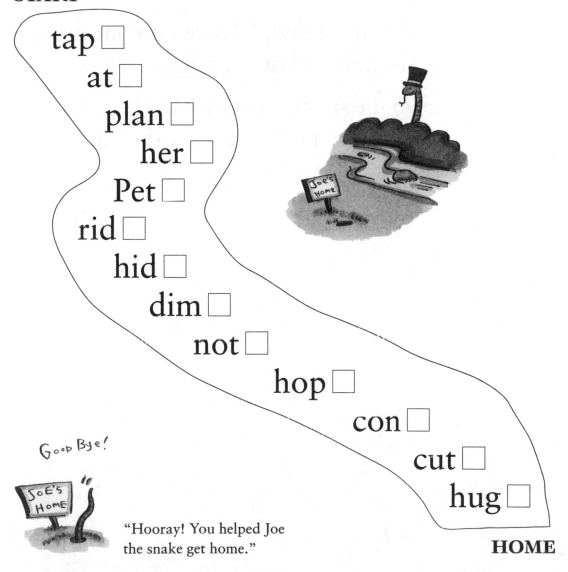

tap ☐

at ☐

plan ☐

her ☐

Pet ☐

rid ☐

hid ☐

dim ☐

not ☐

hop ☐

con ☐

cut ☐

hug ☐

Goop Bye!

Joe's Home

"Hooray! You helped Joe the snake get home."

HOME

Read this poem and circle the silent *e* words.

A snake went down a hole.
He was looking for a mole.

The snake said, "There's no one home."
The mole hid behind a stone.

The snake said, "There's no one here."
The mole shook with fear.

Up the snake went, out of the hole.
Back into his home went the mole.

"What does silent *e* do?" "It makes the vowel in front say its own name."

MY SNAKE   Preteach: does   shake   because

Jake is my snake.
He is black and
   white.

He does not bite.
He makes my sister
   shake

because she is not
   brave.
I am glad he is mine!

CAKE   Preteach: batter   places   tastes

Dave bakes a cake.
He makes batter
   and

puts it in a pan.
Dave places the pan
   in the oven.

The cake is baked.
The cake tastes
   great!

BIKES   Preteach: race   store   should

I like to ride my
   bike.
Steve likes to ride
   his bike.

We race to the lake.
We race to the
   store.
One time his brakes
   broke.

One time my tire
   went flat.
I think we should
   race on skates!

READING SELECTIONS FOR APPENDIX A: CONNECTING SOUND SETS

The best way for your child to apply phonic information is by reading connected print. Here are two suggested books for each phonic set in appendix A. These books can be found at your child's school library or the public library. Happy Reading!

Short *a* Books

Green Eggs and Ham by Dr. Seuss, Beginner Books, distributed by Random House, 1960. Sam-I-Am tries to offer green eggs and ham in a variety of ways: pages 9–12.

Henry and Mudge and the Happy Cat by Cynthia Rylant, Aladdin Books, 1990. Henry and his big dog Mudge find a cat that looks like mashed prunes: pages 7–8.

Short *e* Books

Where Is My Teddy? by Jez Alborough, Candlewick Press, 1992. Eddie goes searching for his lost teddy in the dark woods, and he comes across a huge bear with the same problem.

The Best Nest by P. D. Eastman, Beginner Books, distributed by Random House, 1968. Parent birds search for the perfect nest: pages 3–5.

Short *i* Books

Big Egg by Molly Coxe, Random House, 1997. A mother hen wakes up one morning to find a huge egg in her nest.

It's a Good Thing There Are Insects by Allan Fowler, Children's Press, 1990. This book describes good things that insects can do.

Short *o* Books

Jog, Frog, Jog by Barbara Gregorich, School Zone, 1984. A frog tries to get away from a mean dog.

One fish two fish red fish blue fish by Dr. Seuss, Beginner Books, distributed by Random House, 1960. Lots of animals do crazy antics: pages 38–39.

Short *u* Books

Gum on the Drum by Barbara Gregorich, School Zone, 1984. Gum gets all over when a bear plays the drum.

Mr. Putter and Tabby Walk the Dog by Cynthia Rylant, Scholastic, 1994. The neighbor's dog gives Mr. Putter and Tabby lots of trouble when they take him for walks.

Letter *c* Books

See How They Grow: Calf by Mary Ling, Dorling Kindersley, 1993. See how a calf grows after it is born.

Amelia Bedelia Goes Camping by Peggy Parish, Greenwillow, 1985. Amelia "pitches" tents and other crazy camping antics: pages 13–17.

Letter *g* Books

Jog, Frog, Jog by Barbara Gregorich, School Zone, 1996. A frog has to jog fast to get away from a mean dog.

Good Hunting, Blue Sky by Peggy Parish, Harper & Row, 1989. A young Indian boy goes hunting for food only to have the food bring him home instead: pages 11–16.

ch Books

Chad Checks: The Sound of CH by Peg Ballard, The Child's World, Inc., 2000. Easy to read sentences using ch words.

See How They Grow: Chick by Jane Burton, Dorling Kindersley, 1991. A chick hatches from an egg and grows up.

sh Books

Shoes: The Sound of SH by Peg Ballard, The Children's World, Inc., 2000. Easy to read sentences that use sh words.

One fish two fish red fish blue fish by Dr. Seuss, Beginner Books, distributed by Random House, 1960. One creature after another find themselves in silly situations: pages 56–57.

th Books

This and That: The Sound of TH by Peg Ballard, The Children's World, Inc., 2000. Easy to read sentences that use th words.

Thunderhoof by Syd Hoff, Harper & Row, 1971. A wild horse wants to stay wild, or does he?: pages 15–18.

wh Books

What and Where: The Sound of WH by Robert B. Noyed, The Children's World, Inc., 2000. Easy to read sentences using wh words.

Sam and the Firefly by P. D. Eastman, Beginner Books, distributed by Random House, 1958. A firefly gets into trouble by being naughty: pages 16–19.

ai Books

No Mail for Mitchell by Catherine Siracusa, Random House, 1992. Mitchell the mailman loves to deliver mail, but he is sad because he doesn't get any letters.

Buffalo Bill and the Pony Express by Eleanor Coerr, HarperCollins, 1995. Bill and his horse Bluetail carry the mail past wolves, through storms, and other adventures: pages 20–22.

e a Books

One fish two fish red fish blue fish by Dr. Seuss, Beginner Books, distributed by Random House, 1960. One creature after another find themselves in silly situations: pages 26–27.

Teach us Amelia Bedelia by Peggy Parish, Scholastic, 1977. Amelia Bedelia takes her assignments literally and provides a fun day at school: pages 30–31.

e e Books:

Beep Beep by Barbara Gregorich, School Zone, 1984. A man faces a traffic jam of sheep.

Look at a Tree by Eileen Curran, Troll Associates, 1985. There are lots of things that live around trees.

o o Books

That's Not All by Rex Schneider, School Zone, 1985. Lots of animals cause a ruckus in a lady's house.

Sam and the Firefly by P. D. Eastman, Beginner Books, distributed by Random House, 1958. A firefly gets into trouble by being naughty: pages 6–11.

o u Books

Mouse and Owl by Joan Hoffman, School Zone, 1991. Mouse wants to search for food, but a hungry owl is watching.

Wake Me in Spring by James Preller, Scholastic Hello Readers, 1994. Bear is ready to hibernate but his friend Mouse will miss him.

a r Books

Dark Night, Sleepy Night by Harriet Ziefert, Puffin Books, 1988. Horses sleep standing up and other animals' sleeping habits are illustrated.

Down on the Funny Farm by P. E. King, Random House, 1986. A farmer finds a farm that has very strange animal activities: pages 20–21.

ing Books

One fish two fish red fish blue fish by Dr. Seuss, Beginners Books, distributed by Random House, 1960. One creature after another find themselves in silly situations: page 40.

"Only Joking," Laughed the Lobster by Colin West, Candlewick Press, 1995. A lobster plays practical jokes and gets into trouble.

Letter *b* Books

One Day in the Jungle by Colin West, Candlewick Press, 1995. A butterfly sneezes and sets off a series of sneezes in the jungle.

Because a Little Bug went Ka-Choo! by Rosetta Stone, Beginner Books, distributed by Random House, 1975. A bug sneezes, leading to a parade down the middle of main street.

Letter *d* Books

Jeb's Barn by Andrea Butler, GoodYearBooks, 1994. Each day of the week the Amish community helps to build Jeb's Barn.

Buzz Said the Bee by Wendy Cheyette Lewison, Scholastic, 1992. A bee sits on a duck and creates a commotion.

Silent *e* Books

Smiles: The Sound of Long I by Robert B. Noyed and Cynthia Klingel, The Child's World, Inc., 2000. Easy to read sentences that use silent *e* words.

A Snake Mistake by Mavis Smith, Puffin Books, 1991. A true story about a snake that swallowed some light bulbs.

Reading Rescue Book List

The most valuable tools in teaching a child to read are good books. Books in this list were chosen to appeal to a reader of any age, boy or girl, and are arranged within sections from the easiest books to books with harder-to-read vocabularies. These books are kid-tested by hundreds of children and will make your child laugh, learn, and want to read more.

Easiest-to-Read Books

Sad Dad Bad Had

Dad is sad.

He is very, very sad.

What a bad day Dad had.

         —from *Hop on Pop* by Dr. Seuss, Random House, 1963

These are great books to bolster the emerging reader's self-esteem in reading. Choose three to four sight words to preteach your child using note cards. Then read the book to him using the *To, With, and By* technique (for review, see chapter 4). When he reads these books fluently, he is ready for the next level of books.

Cats: The Sound of Short A by Alice K. Flanagan, The Child's World, Inc., 2000. Easy to read sentences with short a.

Ben's Pens: The Sound of Short E by Alice K. Flanagan, The Child's World, Inc., 2000. Easy to read sentences with short e.

Little Bit: The Sound of Short I by Peg Ballard and Cynthia Klingel, The Child's World, Inc., 2000. Easy to read sentences with short i.

Hot Pot: The Sound of Short O by Alice Flanagan, The Child's World, Inc., 2000. Easy to read sentences with short o.

Fun!: The Sound of Short U by Peg Ballard, The Child's World, Inc., 2000. Easy to read sentences with short u.

Who Ate It? by Taro Gomi, Millbrook Press, 1991. Shows different familiar foods, and reader has to discover which animal ate the food.

My Puppy by Inez Greene, Good Year Books, 1994. A puppy is licking an African-American child.

The Fox on the Box by Barbara Gregorich, School Zone, 1984. Fox has fun playing with a box.

The Gum on the Drum by Barbara Gregorich, School Zone, 1984. Bubble gum makes it hard for a bear to play drums.

Jog, Frog, Jog by Barbara Gregorich, School Zone, 1984. A dog chases a frog that likes to jog.

I Want a Pet by Barbara Gregorich, School Zone, 1984. Boy decides which color pet he likes the best.

Hop on Pop by Dr. Seuss, Random House, 1963. Mr. Brown is upside down, and other funny short stories.

Bob Books by Bobby Lyn Maslen, Scholastic, 1976. Simple stories highlighting short vowels.

A Pet for Pat by Pegeen Snow, Children's Press, 1984. A young child takes a pet dog to the vet.

Mrs. Sato's Hens by Laura Min, Good Year Books, 1994. An Asian woman's hen lays eggs each day of the week.

Easy-to-Read Books

One day in the jungle there was a little sneeze.

"Bless you, Butterfly!" said Lizard.

Next day in the jungle there was a not-quite-so-little sneeze.

"Bless you, Lizard!" said Parrot.

—from *One Day in the Jungle* by Colin West, Candlewick Press, 1995

Choose a short selection from one of these books to read with your child using the *To, With, and By* technique (see chapter 4). Some of these books lend themselves to reading several short selections because of their length. Don't rush through these books—they will be the foundation for your child's success in reading. When she is fluent with these, proceed to the Beginning Readers.

Cat Traps by Molly Coxe, Random House, 1996. A hungry cat tries to catch different animals without success.

Big Egg by Molly Coxe, Random House, 1997. A mother hen wakes up one morning to find a huge egg in her nest.

Go, Dog, Go! by P. D. Eastman, Random House, 1961. Blue and red dogs are busy doing various activities.

The Foot Book by Dr. Seuss, Random House, 1968. You meet slow feet, quick feet, wet feet, and dry feet in this book.

Great Day for Up! by Dr. Seuss, Random House, 1974. Animals and people wake up, get up, and go up when a day starts.

One Day in the Jungle by Colin West, Candlewick Press, 1995. A series of animals sneeze louder and louder until the elephant sneezes away the jungle.

"What is that?" said the Cat by Grace Maccarone, Scholastic, 1995. Animals try different ways to get a big box open and are surprised by what is inside.

Who Loves Me Best? by Kirsten Hall, Reader's Digest Children's Books, 1999. A boy gives lots of hints about his best friend.

Jeb's Barn by Andrea Butler, Good Year Books, 1994. An Amish family spends a week building a barn.

Mouse and Owl by Joan Hoffman, School Zone, 1991. Mouse wants to search for food, but a hungry owl is watching.

Look Closer by Brian and Rebecca Wildsmith, Scholastic, 1993. Search for hidden animals while going on a walk in the outdoors.

Beep, Beep by Barbara Gregorich, School Zone, 1984. Man in truck gets stuck on a road by a flock of sheep.

Cookie's Week by Cindy Ward, Sandcastle Books, 1988. Each day of the week, Cookie the cat gets into trouble around the house.

Gotcha! by Gail Jorgensen, Scholastic, 1995. Bertha Bear chases a beastly fly at her birthday party.

A Polar Bear Can Swim by Harriet Ziefert, Puffin Science Easy-to-Read, 1998. Polar bears can swim, but they can't sleep upside down like bats, and other animal activities.

The Chicken Book by Garth Williams, A Dell Picture Yearling Book, 1970. Chicks want something to eat and momma hen shows them how to get food.

Star Wars, Anakin to the Rescue by Cecilia Venn, Random House, 1999. Young Anakin Skywalker helps a lost boy find his way home.

Beginning Readers

If you give a mouse a cookie, he's going to ask for a glass of milk.

When you give him the milk, he'll probably ask you for a straw.

When he's finished, he'll ask for a napkin.

> —from *If You Give a Mouse a Cookie* by Laura Numeroff,
> Harper & Row, 1985

Often an author has written several good beginning readers. Look in the library or books store for more books written by the same author.

Clifford the Big Red Dog (Series) by Norman Bridwell, Scholastic Inc., 1963. Emily Elizabeth enjoys her very big and very red dog.

Thunderhoof by Syd Hoff, Harper & Row, 1971. Thunderhoof, a wild horse, refuses to be tamed by some cowboys, but changes his mind later on.

Dark Night, Sleepy Night by Harriet Ziefert, Viking Kestrel, 1988. Farm animals sleep at night in many different ways.

Owl Babies by Martin Waddell, Candlewick Press, 1975. Three owl babies whose mother has gone out in the night are worried while she is gone.

Good Hunting, Blue Sky by Peggy Parish, Harper & Row, 1988. A young Indian boy goes hunting for food, only to have the food bring him home instead.

"Pardon?" said the Giraffe by Colin West, Lippincott, 1986. A small frog hops on bigger and bigger animals to finally be heard by a giraffe.

A Snake Mistake by Mavis Smith, HarperCollins, 1991. Farmer Henry uses light bulbs as fake eggs to fool his hens into laying more eggs, and Jake the Snake swallows some light bulbs. A true story.

Going to Sleep on a Farm by Wendy Cheyette Lewison, Dial Books for Young Readers, 1992. At bedtime a father describes for his son how each animal on the farm goes to sleep.

Henry Goes West by Robert Quackenbush, Parents Magazine Press, 1994. Henry the Duck decides to visit Clara who is vacationing out West, and he gets into some trouble.

See How They Grow Fox, Dorling Kindersley, 1992. See what a fox looks like when it is born, and while it grows up.

See How They Grow Pig, Dorling Kindersley, 1993. A piglet is born and grows up to become a sow.

See How They Grow Rabbit, Lodestar, 1991. Learn how a rabbit grows from birth to adult size.

Willie's Wonderful Pet by Mel Cebulash, Scholastic Inc., 1993. Willie brings an unusual pet to school for Pet Day.

Dinosaur Babies by Lucille Recht Penner, Random House, 1991. Describes the characteristics and behavior of baby dinosaurs.

Wake Up Sun! by David L. Harrison, Random House, 1986. Dog wakes up in the middle of the night, and he wakes the other farm animals in a worried search for the sun.

If You Give a Mouse a Cookie by Laura Numeroff, Harper & Row, 1985. If you give a mouse a cookie, all sorts of things are likely to happen.

Dragon Gets By by Dav Pilkey, Orchard Books, 1991. Dragon wakes up groggy and goes through a tough day.

Where's My Teddy? by Jez Alborough, Candlewick Press, 1992. Eddie goes searching for his lost teddy in the dark woods, and he comes across a huge bear with the same problem.

Fortunately by Remy Charlip, Four Winds Press, 1986. Good and bad luck accompany Ned on his way to a surprise birthday party.

Bears Are Curious by Joyce Milton, Random House, 1998. Mother bear comes out of hibernation with new cubs to hunt for food.

The Big Sneeze by Ruth Brown, Lothrop, Lee & Shepard Books, 1985. A farmer sneezes a fly off his nose, and creates a commotion in a barnyard.

One fish, two fish, red fish, blue fish by Dr. Seuss, Random House, 1960. One creature after another find themselves in silly situations.

Wake Me in Spring by James Preller, Scholastic Hello Reader!, 1994. Bear needs to hibernate for the winter, but mouse is sad because he will miss his friend, bear.

A Fish Out of Water by P. D. Eastman, Random House, 1989. A boy fed his fish too much fish food. The fish grew and grew, and he didn't know what to do.

Because a Little Bug Went Ka-CHOO! by Rosetta Stone, Random House, 1975. A bug sneezed, setting off events that end in a huge parade.

Sheepish Riddles by Katy Hall and Lisa Eisenberg, Dial Books for Young Readers, 1996. What do polite lambs say to their mothers? "Thank ewe," and other jokes.

Puppy Riddles by Katy Hall and Lisa Eisenberg, Dial Books for Young Readers, 1998. Where do you take a sick puppy? To the *dog*tor, and other jokes.

Monster Riddles by Louis Phillips, Viking, 1998. What is a monster's favorite summer food? Ice *scream*, and other jokes.

Riddles and More Riddles! by Bennett Cerf, Random House, 1960. What gets lost every time you stand up? Your lap, and other jokes.

Medium Readers and Chapter Books

As soon as it spots something tasty, the chameleon fixes both eyes on its prey and begins to creep forwards—even more slowly than usual.

Then it opens its mouth just a crack, and ... THWAP! Out shoots this amazingly long tongue with a sticky tip at the end, like a piece of well-chewed chewing gum.

—from *Chameleons Are Cool*, by Martin Jenkins, Scholastic, 1997

There are lots of early chapter books available at a bookstore or public library. Many of them are part of a series. If your child likes one, find more books in that series and help him to read them.

Young Abraham Lincoln by Andrew Woods, Troll Associates, 1992. This is a biography of the man who was president of the United States during the Civil War.

Young Harriet Tubman by Anne Benjamin, Troll Associates, 1992. Describes the life of the black woman who helped over 300 slaves escape through the Underground Railroad.

Young Jackie Robinson by Edward Farrell, Troll Associates, 1992. Jackie was the first black player in modern American major league baseball.

Young Rosa Parks by Anne Benjamin, Troll Associates, 1996. Rosie refused to give up her seat on a bus in Montgomery, Alabama, in 1955, leading to a bus boycott that helped to start the civil rights movement.

The Story of Ferdinand by Munro Leaf, Viking Press, 1936. Ferdinand the bull likes to sit quietly and smell flowers. One day he gets stung by a bee, and his stomping convinces bullfighters that he is a fierce bull.

Chameleons Are Cool by Martin Jenkins, Candlewick Press, 1998. Describes chameleons who have long tongues, change colors, and roll their eyes in opposite directions.

My Hen Is Dancing by Karen Wallace, Candlewick Press, 1994. A hen spends a day in the farmyard eating, keeping her feathers clean, and caring for her chicks.

I Love Guinea Pigs by Dick King-Smith, Candlewick Press, 1995. Guinea pigs make great pets and come from Dutch Guiana and other important facts.

S-S-S-Snakes! by Lucille Recht Penner, Random House, 1994. A snake has 400 bones in its back, and a huge snake can swallow a leopard, plus more interesting information.

Abe Lincoln's Hat by Martha Brenner, Random House, 1994. Abraham Lincoln liked to carry official papers in his tall black hat while being a lawyer and then President of the United States.

Star Wars Jar Jar's Mistake by Nancy Krulik, Random House, 1999. Jar Jar Binks has adventures and mishaps in the marketplace on the planet Tatooine.

The Biggest Animal on Land by Allan Fowler, Children's Press, 1996. Describes the elephant as being the largest animal in the zoo.

Gator or Croc? by Allan Fowler, Children's Press, 1996. Alligators are different from crocodiles in a number of ways.

Giant Pandas by Allan Fowler, Children's Press, 1995. Pandas living in China are an endangered species.

Hard-to-See Animals by Allan Fowler, Children's Press, 1997. Try to find animals that are camouflaged in their surroundings.

It Could Still Be a Dinosaur by Allan Fowler, Children's Press, 1993. Dinosaurs are described that lived millions of years ago.

It Could Still Be a Robot by Allan Fowler, Children's Press, 1997. Smart machines perform tasks too dangerous, or too difficult for people to do.

It's Best to Leave a Snake Alone by Allan Fowler, Children's Press, 1992. Describes the physical characteristics and behavior of snakes.

The Bravest Dog Ever: The True Story of Balto by Natalie Standiford, Random House, 1989. Balto, the sled dog saved Nome, Alaska, in 1925 from a diphtheria epidemic by delivering medicine through a raging snowstorm.

Stars by Jennifer Dussling, Grosset & Dunlap, 1996. Stars and what people have thought about them in different times and places are explained.

Mr. Putter and Tabby Walk the Dog (Series) by Cynthia Rylant, Scholastic, 1994. Mr. Putter and his cat Tabby agree to walk the neighbor's dog for a week, not knowing what they are in for.

Fox on the Job (Series) by James Marshall, Puffin Books, 1988. Fox tries to earn money for a new bicycle by working at several different jobs.

The Golly Sisters (Series) *Go West* by Betsy Bryars, Harper Trophy, 1985. May-May and Rose, the singing, dancing Golly sisters, travel west by covered wagon.

Henry and Mudge (Series) *and the Happy Cat* by Cynthia Rylant, Aladdin Books, 1990. Henry and his big dog Mudge find a cat who looks like mashed prunes.

Amelia Bedelia (Series) by Peggy Parish, Harper Trophy, 1963. A literal-minded housekeeper creates havoc in a household by following directions too closely.

Frog and Toad (Series) *Are Friends* by Arnold Lobel, Harper & Row, 1970. It is Spring, and Toad is having a hard time getting out of bed.

ENDNOTES

Introduction

1. U.S. Department of Education, National Center for Educational Statistics, "Executive Summary," of *The 1998 National Assessment for Educational Progress Reading Report Card for the Nation,* NCES 1999-500, P. L. Donahue, K. E. Voelkl, J. R. Campbell, and J. Mazzeo (Washington, D.C.: March 1999).

2. U.S. Department of Education, *Start Early, Finish Strong: How to Help Every Child Become a Reader,* U.S. Department of Education America Reads Challenge (November 1999), 6.

3. Duane Alexander, "The NICHD Research Program in Reading Development, Reading Disorders and Reading Instruction," Keys to Successful Learning: A National Summit on Research in Learning Disabilities, Sponsored by the National Center for Learning Disabilities, (1999): www.ilonline.org/ld_indepth/reading/ncld_summit99.html

4. Bennett Shaywitz, et al., "The Yale Center for the Study of Learning and Attention: Longitudinal and Neurobiological Studies," *Learning Disabilities: A Multidisciplinary Journal* 8, no. 1 (1997): 21–29.

5. G. Reid Lyon, "Overview of Reading and Literacy Research," in *The Keys to Literacy,* Susannah Patton and Madelyn Holmes, eds., (Washington, D.C.: Council for Basic Education, 1998), 10.

6. Barbara Foorman, Jack Fletcher, and David Francis, "Phonics and Literature: the one-two punch that stops reading failure," *Instructor* 108, no. 2 (September 1998): 107.

7. Barbara Swaby, *Diagnosis and Correction of Reading Difficulties* (Boston: Allyn and Bacon, 1989), 121.

8. G. Reid Lyon, "Report on Learning Disabilities Research." Prepared Statement to the Committee on Education and the Workforce, U. S. House of Representatives, *APA Science Advocacy* (July 10, 1997).

Chapter 1

1. Marcia D'Arcangelo, "Learning about Learning to Read: A Conversation with Sally Shaywitz," *Educational Leadership* 57, no. 2 (October 1999): 26–32.

2. U.S. Department of Education, America Reads Challenge, *Start Early, Finish Strong: How to Help Every Child Become a Reader* (Washington, D.C.: 1999), 17.

3. Barbara Swaby, *Diagnosis and Correction of Reading Difficulties* (Boston: Allyn and Bacon, 1989), 31.

Chapter 2

1. Sally Shaywitz, et al., "Functional Disruption in the Organization of the Brain for Reading in Dyslexia," Proceedings of the National Academy of Sciences, 95 (March 1998): 2636–2641.

2. Barbara Kantrowitz and Anne Underwood, "Dyslexia and the New Science of Reading," *Newsweek* (November 22, 1999).

3. Barbara Foorman, Jack Fletcher, and David Francis, "A Scientific Approach to Reading Instruction," LDOnline: the interactive guide to learning disabilities for parents, teachers and children: www.ldonline.org/ld_indepth/reading/cars.html

4. Maria Mody and Richard Schwartz, "Speech Perception and Verbal Memory in Children With and Without Histories of Otitis Media," *Journal of Speech, Language & Hearing Research* 42, no. 5 (October 1999) 1069–1080.

5. Optometrists certified in vision therapy belong to the College of Optometrists in Vision Development (C.O.V.D.)
   P.O. Box 285, Chula Vista, CA 91912-0285
   To find a specialist in your area, call (619) 425-6191.

6. G. Reid Lyon, "Overview of Reading and Literacy Research," in *The Keys to Literacy* (Washington, D.C.: Council for Basic Education, 1998), 6.

7. U.S. Department of Education, National Center for Educational Statistics, "Executive Summary," of *The 1998 National Assessment for Educational Progress Reading Report Card for the Nation*, NCES 1999-500, P. L. Donahue, K. E. Voelkl, J. R. Campbell, and J. Mazzeo (Washington, D.C.: 1999).

Chapter 3

1. Judith W. Paton, "Central Auditory Processing Disorders (CAPD's)": www.ldon-line.org/ld_indepth/process_deficit/capd_paton.html

2. Sandra Cleveland, "Central Auditory Processing Disorder: When Is Evaluation Referral Indicated?" *The ADHD Report* 5, no. 5 (October 1997): 1–7.

Chapter 4

1. Edward Fry, *How to Teach Reading: for Teachers, Parents, Tutors* (Laguna Beach: Laguna Beach Educational Books, 1995), 20.

2. Barbara Swaby, *Diagnosis and Correction of Reading Difficulties* (Boston: Allyn and Bacon, 1989), 99.

3. Edward Fry, *How to Teach Reading: for Teachers, Parents, Tutors* (Laguna Beach: Laguna Beach Educational Books, 1995), 10.

4. Mary Leonhardt, *Parents Who Love Reading, Kids Who Don't: How It Happens and What You Can Do About It* (New York: Crown Publishers, 1993).

5. S. Jay Samuels, "The Method of Repeated Readings," *Reading Teacher* 50, no. 5 (February 1997): 376–381.

6. Barbara Swaby, "Informal Diagnosis and Remediation of Reading," Graduate Course at the University of Colorado at Colorado Springs (1997).

7. Barbara E.R. Swaby, *Journey into Literacy: A Workbook for Parents and Teachers of Young Children,* Colorado Springs: Swaby Books Publisher, 1992.

8. Margaret E. Mooney, *Reading To, With, and By Children,* Katonah, New York: Richard C. Owen Publishers, Inc., 1990.

Chapter 5

1. Barbara Swaby, "Informal Diagnosis and Remediation of Reading," Graduate Course at the University of Colorado at Colorado Springs (1997).

Chapter 13

1. G. Reid Lyon, "Why Johnny Can't Decode," *The Washington Post* (October 27, 1996).

Chapter 14

1. Steve Newman, "Earthweek: A Diary of the Planet*," The Los Angeles Times Syndicate. 2000 Earth Environment Service* (March 25, 2000).

2. Barbara Swaby, *Diagnosis and Correction of Reading Difficulties* (Boston: Allyn and Bacon, 1989), 239.

3. Ibid., 121.

Chapter 15

1. National Center on Education and the Economy, *Nation's Top Literacy Experts Set Out Reading and Writing Targets for Youngest Students,* Primary Literacy Standards Press Release (Washington, D.C.: May 25, 1999).

2. Marge Scherer, "Perspectives/Making Connections," *Educational Leadership* 56, no. 3 (November 1998): 7.

Chapter 16

1. Barbara Swaby, *Diagnosis and Correction of Reading Difficulties* (Boston: Allyn and Bacon, 1989), 265.

2. Quote is from the *Reading Teacher's Book of Lists* by Edward Fry, Copyright © 1993. Reprinted with permission of Prentice Hall Direct.

Chapter 19

1. Edward Fry, *How to Teach Reading: for Teachers, Parents, Tutors* (Laguna Beach: Laguna Beach Educational Books, 1995), 20.

Chapter 20

1. National Institute of Child Health and Human Development, *Report of the National Reading Panel: Teaching Children to Read* (April 13, 2000): www.nichd.nih.gov/publications/nrp.intro.htm

2. National Research Council, "Chapter 6, Instructional Strategies for Kindergarten and the Primary Grades," in *Preventing Reading Difficulties in Young Children,* Catherine Snow, M. Susan Burns, Peg Griffin, eds., (Washington, D.C.: National Academy Press, 1998), 22.

3. Emily Dickinson, "There is no frigate like a book," *101 Great American Poems* (Mineola: Dover Publications, Inc., 1998), 32.

4. William Miller, *Richard Wright and the Library Card* (New York: Scholastic, 1997), dedication page.

Chapter 21

1. Judith W. Paton, "Central Auditory Processing Disorders (CAPD's)," www.ldon-line.org/ld_indepth/process_deficit/capd_paton.html

2. Sandra Cleveland, "Central Auditory Processing Disorder: When Is Evaluation Referral Indicated?" *The ADHD Report 5,* no. 5 (October 1997): www.ldonline.org/ld_indepth/process_deficit/adhdreport_capd.html

3. Judith W. Paton, "Central Auditory Processing Disorders (CAPD's)," www.ldon-line.org/ld_indepth/process_deficit/capd_paton.html

4. Barbara Swaby, "Informal Diagnosis and Remediation of Reading," Graduate Course at the University of Colorado at Colorado Springs (1997).

5. U.S. Department of Education, *Start Early, Finish Strong: How to Help Every Child Become a Reader,* U.S. Department of Education America Reads Challenge (November 1999), 61.

BIBLIOGRAPHY

"ABC's of LD/ADD: Learning Disabilities (LD) and Attention Deficit Disorder (ADD)." Learning Disabilities Online: the interactive guide to learning disabilities for parents, teachers and children: www.ldonline.org/abcs_info/articles-info.html

Alexander, Duane. "The NICHD Research Program in Reading Development, Reading Disorders and Reading Instruction." Keys to Successful Learning: A National Summit on Research in Learning Disabilities. Sponsored by the National Center for Learning Disabilities (1999): www.ilonline.org/ld_indepth/reading/ncld_summit99.html

Brownell, Mary T., and Chriss Walther-Thomas. "Candace Bos: Informed, Flexible Teaching—A Key to Successful Readers." *Intervention in School & Clinic* 34, no. 5 (May 1999): 309–315.

Carbo, Marie. "Whole Language or Phonics? Use Both!" *Education Digest* 61, no. 6 (February 1996): 60–64.

Chard, David J., and Shirley V. Dickson. "Phonological Awareness: Instructional and Assessment Guidelines." *Intervention in School and Clinic* 34, no. 5 (May 1999): 261–270.

Chard, David J., and Jean Osborn. "Phonics and Word Recognition Instruction in Early Reading Programs: Guidelines for Accessibility." A Publication of the Division for Learning Disabilities, Council for Exceptional Children (1999): www.ldonline.org/ld_indepth/reading/ldrp_chard_guidelines.html

Clay, Marie M. *Reading Recovery: A Guidebook for Teachers in Training*. Auckland, NZ: Heinemann, 1993.

Cleveland, Sandra. "Central Auditory Processing Disorder: When Is Evaluation Referral Indicated?" *The ADHD Report* 5, no. 5 (October 1997): 1–7.

Council for Exceptional Children. "Reading Difficulties versus Learning Disabilities." *Council for Exceptional Children Today* 4, no. 5 (Nov/Dec 1997): www.ldonline.org/ld_indepth/reading/cec_rdld.html

D'Arcangelo, Marcia. "Learning about Learning to Read: A Conversation with Sally Shaywitz." *Educational Leadership* 57, no. 2 (October 1999): 26–32.

Dreher, Nancy. "ADD: Tracking the Deficit." *Current Health* 25, no. 1 (September 1998): 27–30.

Edelen-Smith, Patricia J. "How Now Brown Cow: Phoneme Awareness Activities for Collaborative Classrooms." *Intervention in School and Clinic* 33, no. 2 (November 1997): 103–111.

Fletcher, Jack M., Sally Shaywitz, and Bennett Shaywitz. "Comorbidity of Learning and Attention Disorders: Separate but Equal." *Pediatric Clinics of North America* 46, no. 5 (October 1999): 885–895.

Foorman, Barbara, Jack Fletcher, and David Francis. "Phonics and Literature: the one-two punch that stops reading failure." *Instructor* 108, no. 2 (September 1998): 107.

———. "A Scientific Approach to Reading Instruction." Learning Disabilities Online: the interactive guide to learning disabilities for parents, teachers and children: *www.ldonline.org/ld_indepth/reading/cars.html*

Fry, Edward. *How to Teach Reading: for Teachers, Parents, Tutors*. Laguna Beach: Laguna Beach Educational Books, 1995.

Fry, Edward, Jacqueline Kress, and Dona Lee Fountoukidis. *The Reading Teacher's Book of Lists*. 3rd ed. Paramus, NJ: Prentice Hall, Inc. 1993.

Gaskins, Irene W., and Linnea C. Ehri. "Procedures for Word Learning: Making Discoveries about Words." *Reading Teacher* 50, no. 4 (Dec 96/Jan 97): 312–328.

Hall, Susan L. "Report of the National Reading Panel: Teaching Children to Read." Learning Disabilities Online: the interactive guide to learning disabilities for parents, teachers and children (April 2000): www.ldonline.org/ld_indepth/reading/teaching_children_to_read.html

Juel, Connie, and Cecilia Minden-Cupp. "One Down and 80,000 to Go: Word Recognition Instruction in the Primary Grades." *Reading Teacher* 53, no. 4 (Dec 99/Jan 2000): 332–337.

Kantrowitz, Barbara, and Anne Underwood. "Dyslexia and the New Science of Reading." *Newsweek* (November 22, 1999): 72–78.

Lally, Kathy, and Debbie M. Price. "Learning How We Read." *Palm Beach Post*. West Palm Beach, Florida (January 4, 1998): plA+.

Learning First Alliance. "Every Child Reading: An Action Plan." A Learning First Alliance Action Paper, Washington, D.C. (June 1998): www.learningfirst.org/readingaction.html

Leonhardt, Mary. *Parents Who Love Reading, Kids Who Don't: How It Happens and What You Can Do About It*. New York: Crown Publishers, 1993.

Liberman, Isabell, and Donald Shankweiler, "The Alphabetic Principle and Learning to Read." U.S. Department of Health and Human Services 717, no. 22 (1993): 1–33.

Lindblom, Mike. "Decoding the Mystery of Dyslexia." *The Seattle Times* (January 12, 1999): A6.

Lyon, G. Reid. "From Letters to Sounds." *The Washington Post* (October 27, 1996).

———. "Why Johnny Can't Decode." *The Washington Post* (October 27, 1996).

———. "Report on Learning Disabilities Research." Prepared Statement to the Committee on Education and the Workforce. U. S. House of Representatives. *APA Science Advocacy* (July 10, 1997).

Mastropieri, Margo A., Amy Leinart, and Thomas E. Scruggs. "Strategies to Increase Reading Fluency." *Intervention in School & Clinic* 34, no. 5 (May 1999): 278–285.

Moats, Louisa C. *Teaching Reading Is Rocket Science*. Washington, D.C.: American Federation of Teachers, June 1999.

Mody, Maria, and Richard Schwartz. "Speech Perception and Verbal Memory in Children With and Without Histories of Otitis Media." *Journal of Speech, Language & Hearing Research* 42, no. 5 (October 1999): 1069–1080.

Murray, Bruce, and Theresa Lesnick. "The Letterbox Lesson: A Hands-On Approach for Teaching Decoding." *Reading Teacher* 52, no. 6 (March 1999): 644–651.

National Association of School Psychologists. "Special Edition: Attention Problems." *Communique* (spring 2000).

National Center on Education and the Economy. *Nation's Top Literacy Experts Set Out Reading and Writing Targets for Youngest Students*. Primary Literacy Standards Press Release (Washington, D.C.: May 25, 1999).

National Institute of Child Health and Human Development. *Report of the National Reading Panel: Teaching Children to Read* (April 13, 2000): www.nichd.nih.gov/publications/nrp.intro.htm

National Research Council. *Preventing Reading Difficulties in Young Children*. Catherine Snow, M. Susan Burns, Peg Griffin, eds. Washington, D.C.: National Academy Press, 1998.

Paton, Judith W. "Central Auditory Processing Disorders (CAPD's)." Learning Disabilities Online: the interactive guide to learning disabilities for parents, teachers and children: www.ldonline.org/ld_indepth/process_deficit/capd_paton.html

Patton, Susannah, and Madelyn Holmes, eds. *The Keys to Literacy* Washington, D.C.: Council for Basic Education, 1998.

Rasinski, Timothy V., and Nancy Padak. "Effects of Fluency Development on Urban Second-Grade Readers." *Journal of Educational Research* 87, no. 3 (Jan/Feb 1994): 158–166.

Samuels, S. Jay. "The Method of Repeated Readings." *Reading Teacher* 50, no. 5 (February 1997): 376–381.

Scherer, Marge. "Perspectives/Making Connections." *Educational Leadership* 56, no. 3 (November 1998): 7.

Shaywitz, Sally. "Dyslexia." *Scientific American* 275, no. 5 (Nov. 1996): 98–105.

———. "Dyslexia." *New England Journal of Medicine* 338, no. 5 (January 29, 1998): 307–312.

Shaywitz, Bennett, et al. "The Yale Center for the Study of Learning and Attention: Longitudinal and Neurobiological Studies." *Learning Disabilities: A Multidisciplinary Journal* 8, no. 1 (1997): 21–29.

Shaywitz, Sally, et al. "Functional Disruption in the Organization of the Brain for Reading in Dyslexia." *Proceedings of the National Academy of Sciences* 95 (March 1998): 2636–2641.

Simyak, Helen B. "Sounding Off on 'Sounding Out': Why should we rethink the way we teach phonics?" *Reading Today* 14, no. 4 (Feb/Mar 1997): 32–36.

Stahl, Steven A., Ann Duffy-Hester, et al. "Everything You Wanted to Know about Phonics (But Were Afraid to Ask)." *Reading Research Quarterly* 33, no. 3 (July–September 1998): 338–356.

Stark, Rachel E., and John M. Heinz. "Vowel Perception in Children with and without Language Impairment." *Journal of Speech & Hearing Research* 39, no. 4 (August 1996): 860–870.

Strickland, Dorothy S. "What's Basic in Beginning Reading? Finding Common Ground." *Educational Leadership* 55, no. 6 (March 1998): 6–11.

Swaby, Barbara E.R. *Teaching and Learning Reading: A Pragmatic Approach.* Boston: Little, Brown and Company, 1984.

———. *Diagnosis and Correction of Reading Difficulties.* Boston: Allyn and Bacon, 1989.

———. *Journey into Literacy: A Workbook for Parents and Teachers of Young Children.* Colorado Springs: Swaby Books Publisher, 1992.

U.S. Department of Education. *Start Early, Finish Strong: How to Help Every Child Become a Reader.* U.S. Department of Education America Reads Challenge. Washington, D.C.: November 1999.

U.S. Department of Education, National Center for Educational Statistics. *The Executive Summary of the 1998 National Assessment for Educational Progress Reading Report Card for the Nation.* NCES 1999–500. P. L. Donahue, K. E. Voelkl, J. R. Campbell, and J. Mazzeo Washington, D.C.: March 1999.

Wartik, Nancy, and Lavonne Carlson-Finnerty. *Memory and Learning.* New York: Chelsea House Publishers, 1993.

Index